heart-felt WOOL APPLIQUÉ

LORINDA LIE

American Quilter's Society

P. O. Box 3290 • Paducah, KY 42002-3290
e-mail: info@AQSquilt.com

Located in Paducah, Kentucky, the American Quilter's Society (AQS) is dedicated to promoting the accomplishments of today's quilters. Through its publications and events, AQS strives to honor today's quiltmakers and their work and to inspire future creativity and innovation in quiltmaking.

EDITOR: DIANE SCHNECK

TECHNICAL EDITOR: BARBARA SMITH

BOOK DESIGN/ILLUSTRATIONS: LYNDA SMITH

COVER DESIGN: MICHAEL BUCKINGHAM

PHOTOGRAPHY: CHARLES R. LYNCH

Library of Congress Cataloging-in-Publication Data

> Lie, Lorinda.
>> Heart-felt wool appliqué / Lorinda Lie.
>>> p. cm.
>> Includes bibliographical references.
>> ISBN 1-57432-750-X
>> 1. Appliqué--Patterns. 2. Quilting--Patterns. 3. Felt I. Heart-felt wool appliqué
>> TT779 .L53 2000
>>> 746.44'5041--dc21
>>>> 00-009592

Additional copies of this book may be ordered from the American Quilter's Society, PO Box 3290, Paducah, KY 42002-3290 @ $22.95. Add $3.00 for postage and handling.

Acknowledgments

I am indebted to so many people who helped me reach this point in my life and quilting career, with special thanks to my parents, who encouraged creativity in our home, and especially my mother, who taught me to sew.

I thank Jo Fifield, who was my partner in Shared Ideas when we taught our first wool appliqué workshops. Not only did she help me teach classes, she was my devil's advocate and my best friend. Her insights have added greatly to my knowledge of quilts. Thanks for sharing your talents with me and for hand quilting FAN DANCE.

This book could not have been accomplished without the special help and encouragement from all my friends from the Cable Car Quilters Guild in Dubuque, Iowa, who gave me their support and encouragement, came to workshops, made projects, and edited and proofread the manuscript. I give special thanks to Cyndy Billmeyer, Sue Clemens, and Jo Fifield, who helped me edit and proof the manuscript; the pillow makers Sue Clemens, Jean Glise, Deb Jaeger, Marie Jannette, Kathy Napientek, and Barb Scoggin; and Peg Reis, who quilted FALLING LEAVES for me.

As a beginner at machine appliqué, I am indebted to Kathy Napientek for sharing her expertise in machine work. We worked together to adapt general appliqué rules to wool. I am also indebted to Husqvarna Viking. They graciously loaned me two machines to practice on and to develop guidelines for machine-quilting. Oreck Plus in Dubuque, Iowa, generously allowed Kathy to use a couple of machines so we could coordinate our projects across the miles.

I learned about stuffed bindings from Klaudeen Hansen in one of the first workshops I ever took. Many years later, I used that idea to develop my own method.

I would like to thank Bonnie Browning and Lois Arnold, both former members of the Cable Car Quilters Guild, for their continued friendship and support. You helped me through the process.

I would be remiss if I did not thank my husband, Toralf, and my son, Hank. They put up with that wet sheep smell as the wool dried and didn't complain too much when I ripped garments apart while watching TV. They offered support and criticism when it was needed, and best of all, they love sleeping under the wool quilts.

Last but not least I thank all the people at AQS who worked on my book and made it happen. Dreams do come true!

Contents

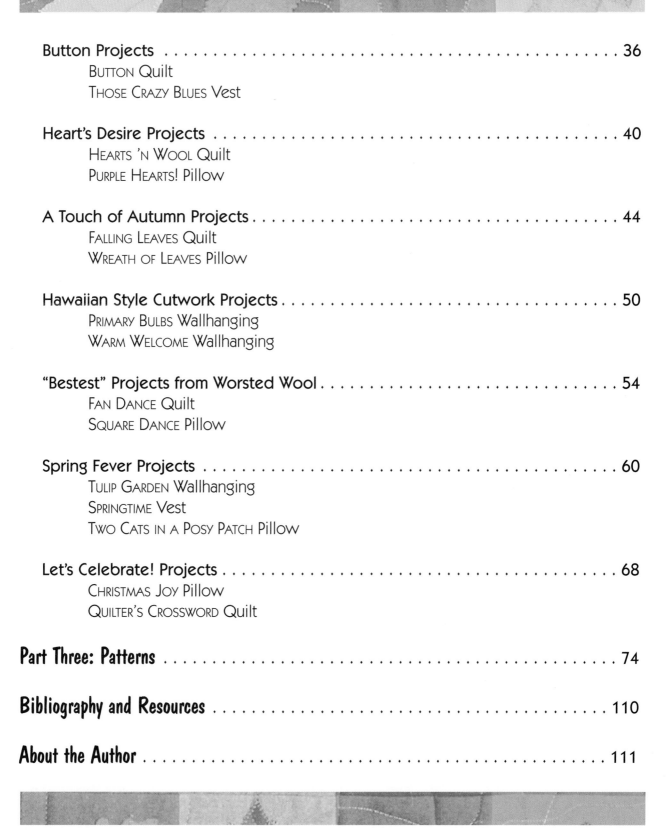

Introduction

Explore the wondrous sensuality of wool as a quilting medium. Its many colors can be soft and alluring, lush or bold, even garish on occasion. The textures are interesting and varied. The weight and the fiber content of wool and wool blends increase its versatility and, at the same time, make it a challenging medium to work with.

Making wool quilts is fun, quick, and easy, and the quilts are warm. These simple designs are elegant to look at and relaxing to do. Wool appliqué is the easiest appliqué technique of all. There are no edges to be turned, no fusing, no fussing, no worrying about reversing shapes or using the right side of the fabric. The blanket stitch makes a perfect finish, and done by hand or machine, it finishes the edge and becomes an integral part of the design. Appliquéd block by block, these are ideal projects to carry around in your purse to work on in all those places you spend your time waiting.

Wool speaks not only to the senses but also to the heart. My first introduction to wool quilts was a dark and heavy quilt pieced of simple squares and tied with red yarn. Mom and Dad slept on the quilt when our family went camping. My grandmother made this quilt from my grandfather's suits. While the quilt did not survive all the camping trips, the memories live on.

My next encounter with wool quilts came through visits to antique shops. Occasionally, I would see penny rugs, table mats, and pin cushions made of layers of wool on wool, all carefully blanket stitched by hand. The little "tongues" of wool around the edges framed many of the pieces with a kind of giant fringe. They were practical pieces, designed for everyday use. We know wool endures because these pieces have survived despite regular usage and storage in attics and basements.

Perhaps that's part of the attraction of wool quilts. They draw us back to the tradition of making quilts from worn-out clothing and remind us of our pioneer roots. The quilts in this book continue that pioneer tradition of recycling wool garments, but with a modern twist.

Most of the projects are made with wool fabric recycled from used clothing, purchased in resale shops, thrift stores, and garage sales, or found on closet shelves and in attics and basements. For those with an adventuresome soul and the collecting spirit, the search for wool is a fun treasure hunt. Wool is an ideal medium for the economically and ecologically minded quilter.

Consider some of the special properties of this fiber. It is flame resistant. This doesn't mean it won't burn, but it is slow to catch fire and burns with a dry ash, unlike synthetics that melt as they burn. A wool quilt with a natural fiber batting will be safer for children.

Heart-Felt Wool Appliqué — Lorinda Lie

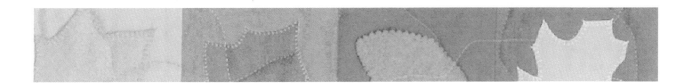

Wool breathes, making it feel cool in the summer and warm in the winter. It can absorb up to 30 percent of its own weight in moisture and still feel dry to the touch; when a garment or quilt feels wet, it also feels cold. Because it is such an absorbent fiber, wool dyes easily and keeps its color. Absorbent fibers don't collect static. Static is what attracts lint, dust, and dirt, so wool is easier to keep clean. If it ever does collect static, hang the garment or quilt in a steamy bathroom to absorb more moisture.

As far as wool allergies are concerned, in teaching many wool appliqué workshops I have only encountered one person who had a true allergic reaction to wool. Many students reported that they couldn't wear wool or were allergic to it, but they were able to handle the felted wool with no difficulty. I have been told that people may be allergic to the chemicals used in the commercial processing of wool or to the lanolin or dander in the wool. The felting process removes these.

Sometimes, what people call an allergy is really a reaction to the prickliness of some wool fibers. The wool used in suits and skirts is generally finer, softer, and less prickly than coarser wool or fuzzier yarn. The felting process also helps because it mats the fibers firmly together. If you are concerned, try out a small project, like one of the pillows, before investing in a larger quilt.

Wool does need to be handled a little differently than quilting cottons. Acquiring a stash is done differently, too. That's all part of the fun.

Heart-Felt Wool Appliqué is a start-to-finish, how-to book based on my experiences in collecting and quilting wool. The first part will give you the best sources for acquiring wool and show you how to prepare it to use in washable quilts. This section will also explore piecing and appliqué. The book provides an in-depth guide to beautiful hand blanket stitches and fancy stitch variations as well as instructions for machine blanket stitches. Instructions are given for appliquéing points that stay in place and for finishing your projects. In addition, the special challenges of working with both recycled and new wool will be explored.

The second part of the book gives complete instructions for making more than a dozen projects for both the beginner and the intermediate quilter. These projects can be done by either hand or machine. The third part includes template patterns for all the projects.

Come, have an adventure with wool!

Heart-Felt Wool Appliqué — Lorinda Lie

Part One: Learning the Basics

Detail from HEARTS 'N WOOL

Collecting Wool

Sources for wool: new or used

Primary sources for wool will depend on whether you choose new or used wool. Larger quilt stores are beginning to carry small selections of wool year around. General fabric stores, particularly the larger chains, will have a broader selection of fabrics to choose from seasonally. Prices vary depending on quality, blend, weight, and season. Expect to pay at least twice as much, or more, for a yard of wool as you would for a yard of top-quality quilting cotton.

Generally, expect a choice of about a half dozen solids and another half dozen plaids. Navy, black, red, gray, forest green, and camel are usually readily available in the fall and winter. Expect most of the colors to be dark.

Do not be tempted to buy craft felt. Quilt stores and general fabric and craft stores carry synthetic felt in a broad range of colors. Once you have worked with wool, you will never again be tempted to use felt for a quilt or garment. It simply does not have the richness, softness, or drape of true felted wool.

True wool felt is a nonwoven fabric made by heating, agitating, washing, and pressing loose wool fibers so they mat together and become interlocked. Felted-wool fabric is made by shrinking the woven wool in a washer and dryer. It is the heat, agitation, friction, and pressure that shrink wool, not the water. Instructions are given on page 11 for felting woven wool. Most wool can be safely hand washed in lukewarm water, if it is not twisted, wrung out, agitated, or pounded.

When it comes to collecting wool, you aren't limited to quilt shops and fabric stores. Begin your hunt in your own closet, basement, and attic. Let your friends, relatives, and colleagues know that you are looking for cast-off wool garments and yard goods. Explain that the garments don't have to be wearable, in mint condition, or even clean.

Next, visit local resale and consignment shops. To find them, check your phone book yellow pages under "consignment," "clothing – consignment," "secondhand," "thrift," and "resale." All of these headings may carry other listings. If you know the specific name of a store, such as Goodwill or Salvation Army, it will be listed in the white pages. Be aware that many of these stores operate on a cash-only basis.

Consignment stores tend to have higher prices than thrift stores. You will find the least expensive garments at charity resale and thrift shops. Visit often, because new stock comes in daily. You will also learn each store's system of markdowns, sales, and bag days (a grocery bagful for a dollar or two).

Other sources for wool include garage and rummage sales. The prices will vary with the owner's attachment to the garment. You can often get a lower price by making an offer or going later in the day. People are more apt to bargain when they want a quick sale. What do you have to lose by asking?

Choosing usable garments

The ideal garment to collect is a 100% wool gathered skirt in a large size. A single skirt may yield more than a yard of fabric for a few dollars. Pleated skirts will also yield greater yardage, though they can be more time-consuming to take apart. Gored skirts have more seams and may not have large enough areas of seamless wool for your purpose. You will soon develop your own preferences about what you want to collect.

Check out the sections of pants, dresses, suits, jackets, and even sweaters. While these may not be your first choices to take apart, they may be just the color or texture you need. You may find more rich and earthy browns, greens, and tweeds in the men's sections. The women's sections tend to have brighter colors, whites, plaids, and pastels.

Women's jackets probably present the greatest challenge to take apart. They tend to be tailored with many seams, interfacings, padding, and so on. They are messy, do not yield large amounts of fabric, and are more expensive. However, it has often been a women's jacket that added just the perfect highlight to a project.

Stick to dress- and pant-weight wools. Coat and blanket weights are too heavy to handle in the projects given here or to use with other lighter weight wool fabrics.

Wool comes in a great variety of weaves from very fine to fairly loose. The looser the weave, the higher you want the wool content. Even in 100% wool, some weaves will require a little extra care. They may also have a slightly more ragged finish as you appliqué them.

Some wool that appears to be very loosely woven will felt into a very compact weave. Others will not. Crepes, worsted wool, and gabardines are tight, fine weaves. The latter are the weaves often found in men's suits and trousers. They felt less and ravel more than other wool weaves. Save these pieces for pieced projects like the FAN DANCE quilt on page 54.

The most common colors to find in used clothing are red, navy, black, gray, and camel. A wide range of pinks, purples, greens, and blues, as well as more unusual colors like apricot and chartreuse are out there if you look long enough.

One of the rarer colors is yellow. It is sometimes available as yard goods, and it is handy to have in your collection. Watch for sales and add at least a small piece of yellow to your wool stash when you can.

Fabric content

As you look at garments, check the labels for fabric content. Most of the time you will find wool garments labeled with the symbols shown in Figure 1. These are symbols for quality wool. For best results, purchase wool yardage and garments that are 80% to 100% wool. These will felt most successfully and ravel the least. Do

not buy a garment that is not labeled because correctly guessing a garment's fabric content is impossible. Many fabrics that have the look and feel of wool are imposters. As you gain more experience with purchased garments, you may be able to make some educated guesses based on the manufacturer, but not always.

WOOLMARK BLEND   WOOLMARK

Figure 1. Fabric content symbols.

The lower the wool content, the less the fabric will felt or shrink and the more it will tend to fray as you work with it. Most of the time, the piece isn't worth the hassle. However, if the color is perfect and it is worth the potential extra work, take a risk and try felting. Two or three dollars isn't really much of a risk if you decide to discard a garment in the end. Once you get an unlabeled garment home, either go ahead and felt it (described on page 11) and see if it ravels easily, or try one of the following tests before making your decision to discard or keep the garment.

Tests for Fiber Content
Burn test
Unravel a few threads of wool fabric. Hold the threads with tweezers over a metal tin so you don't burn your fingers. When lit with a match, 100% wool fibers burn slowly with a small flame that will go out when the match is removed. Burning leaves a dry, dusty ash.

A wool blend will burn quickly with a larger flame. When the match is put out, the fibers will continue to burn. When the flame is extinguished, the resulting bead will feel hard, like plastic.

Bleach test
Put a small piece of wool in a glass of undiluted chlorine bleach. It will dissolve in about an hour. If the piece of fabric is a blend, the wool will dissolve, leaving a woven framework of other fibers. You will get a rough idea of the percentage of wool by gauging the amount of fiber that dissolved.

Heart-Felt Wool Appliqué — Lorinda Lie

Preparing Wool for Use

Cleaning wool

Now that you have all these garments or yardages, what do you do with them? Consider the source. Take all your recycled garments to your laundry area and either felt them immediately or leave them there until you are ready to work with them. Do not take them to your sewing area or other parts of your house until they are clean. Garments from thrift stores, garage sales, attics, and basements routinely come "as is." The wool may be dirty and have bugs or eggs. You do not want to risk infecting other garments or fibers in your home, such as drapes, carpets, or your best wool suit.

Felting wool

Felting is the process that shrinks the wool, mats the woven fibers together, and eliminates raveling. This process happens through the combination of heat, agitation, and pressure in your washer and dryer. It makes old clothes into quilting fabric.

Color sort lights and darks, placing like colors together. For example, put red and purple in one pile, brown, navy, and black in another, and white, pale pink, and camel in a third pile. If you don't have enough garments to make a small washer load, get together with a friend who is also collecting wool and combine your loads. Separate yours from hers by putting a safety pin through a belt loop in your garments, or wait until you have several more garments collected and then do a load. If you are felting wool yardage, trim off the selvages before washing. These edges will not felt like the rest of the yardage because of the difference in weave, causing uneven felting and stretching.

Wash the garments on your longest, hottest wash cycle with the highest agitation and a mild detergent. Use a moderate water level because you want to crowd the garments. This will shrink the wool and mat the fibers together to felt it. One long, hot washing cycle should be enough. Use the cold water rinse cycle to check for colorfastness. Dry on your longest, hottest drying cycle.

Checking colorfastness

If you are making primarily dark or monochromatic quilts, like the Button quilts, page 36, and Hearts 'n Wool, page 40, you do not need to be overly concerned about colors bleeding. Bleeds won't show on the dark colors.

If you will be mixing lights and darks in your quilt and you are concerned about bleeding, check the wash and rinse waters. Generally, reds will bleed the most, but other colors will bleed too. If you notice bleeding in the hot wash-cycle, complete the cycle and check the cold rinse cycle. Some wools bleed only in hot water.

If a fabric still bleeds in the cold rinse, dry the wool. The colors may heat-set in the dryer. After the wool is dry, cut off the waistbands of the skirts or pants and remove the lining. Sometimes it is not the wool but the lining that is bleeding. Take each garment and wet it in cold water. If the water runs clear, that garment can be used. Because you will be washing your finished quilt with a short, delicate cold cycle, you need be concerned only about cold water bleeds.

If a garment is still bleeding, try one of these options: Wash it in vinegar and salt or a commercial dye setting product, discard the garment, or put it aside to use with dark or similar colors. Be sure to mark this piece so it doesn't get mixed in with your other tested wool.

I have found that there is no way to predict which garments will bleed. Even a top-line garment may not be colorfast. You have to decide on your own tolerance. I consider the wool quilts in this book to be folk quilts or utility quilts. A minimal amount of bleeding does not worry me, and I have had few problems with it.

Fire hazard

Be sure to empty the lint trap on your dryer every load because it will fill fast.

Unsewing garments

Once the garments are clean and felted, take them to your sewing area. Snip off all the buttons and set them aside to use for embellishments on your quilts. If you haven't already, cut the waistbands off the skirts and pants and discard them along with the linings. Rough cut around zippers and pockets. Save wool pocket pieces for appliqué. Take apart seams, pleats, darts, and hems. Often, you can run an open scissors down the seam, which will cut the stitches without cutting the fabric (Figure 2). Use a fine seam ripper and work carefully to take out darts and pleats without leaving holes in the fabric.

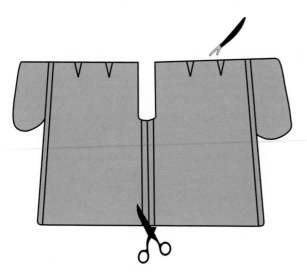

Figure 2. Use a seam ripper for darts. Run an open scissors down the seam to cut sections apart.

Unsewing garments is a messy job, especially working with women's jackets. It is truly amazing how much material is used to pad shoulders. It isn't necessary to remove all the ironed-on interfacing on women's jacket fronts. Use the right side of these pieces for appliqué. After cutting apart one or two jackets, you may decide they aren't worth the effort unless it contains a must-have color. If you have purchased suits, you may want to set the jackets and vests aside before felting. Decorate them for your own use or to give as gifts .

Pressing wool

Lift the iron and press without moving the iron back and forth, which may stretch the wool out of shape. Always press wool with moisture to avoid damaging the fibers. Moisture also helps to remove resistant creases. Use steam, or iron with a damp pressing cloth. To get out stubborn pleats or darts, daub the wool with a wet cloth, or spray the wool with water and then press.

A clapper may be helpful for removing persistent creases and pressing seams open. A clapper is a wood block that you press or "clap" down on a crease or seam to hold the steam in the wool for a few seconds longer after the iron is lifted. To use the clapper, press a section and then place the clapper over the section and hold it in place a few seconds. It is not necessary to slam the clapper down. Firm pressure works just as well. Clappers are available through many of the sewing-supply catalogs.

Remember, wool is an animal product, not a plant fiber like cotton or linen. Wool is like your hair. Curly hair takes moisture and heat to straighten, straight hair takes moisture and heat to curl. Hair that is too dry gets brittle. The same is true for wool.

Because garments are felted before they are taken apart, there may be some unevenness or rippling, particularly where there was a pleat or dart. Don't worry about it. This is part of the folk look of recycled wool. Think of how people use jeans in quiltmaking, incorporating rivets, belt loops, pockets, and seams into their designs. Use your wool in the same way. If the piece lies flat, you may not want to bother with removing small darts, just incorporate them into your design.

Storing wool

Store your wool clean. This doesn't guarantee you won't get moths, but it lessens the chances, because there won't be any food stains to attract them. Avoid using mothballs because of their strong odor. There are other commercial products available for storing wool. Some of these may be equally strongly scented even if they are herbal. An elderly friend shared with me her solution of storing her wool things with cloves. She buys them in bulk at a natural food store. Her wool things smell wonderful and stay bug free.

General Project Directions

Sizing quilts

Don't get carried away with your projects. It is easy to get on a roll making blocks and end up with a project that is too large for a wool quilt. Most of the projects in this book are relatively small. There are no king-sized quilts for a reason. Wool gets very heavy very fast, particularly wool that is heavily appliquéd, such as the HEARTS 'N WOOL quilt, page 40. Make two smaller topper quilts instead. This is a versatile size that works as a TV throw, dorm quilt, or personal quilt on a shared bed; often, partners don't have the same thermostat.

Cutting blocks

Once you have decided on a project, picked out the wool, and felted it, it's time to cut the blocks. Cut smaller pieces of wool, such as sleeves, pant legs, and skirt backs into blocks (Figure 3). Save the larger, unseamed skirt fronts for projects with larger blocks like the Hawaiian-style cutwork wallhangings on pages 50 and 52. Cut the blocks with your rotary cutter. Use a sharp blade so loose fibers aren't driven into your mat. As you cut the squares or rectangles, save scraps of reasonable size for appliqué or other projects.

Because of the bulk of the wool and the uneven weights of different pieces, right-angle shapes, such as squares and rectangles, are easier to work with than other shapes, particularly for first-time wool users.

If there is fraying as you cut the blocks, it may be because the fabric is a blend, worsted wool, or loose weave. If fraying is slight, treat the fabric very gently. If the fraying is more pronounced, overcast stitch the edges, serge them, or discard the piece. A fray sealant is an option for appliqué pieces, though it tends to make the edges stiff.

Appliqué

All of the projects were appliquéd before the blocks were sewn together. When blocks are small, they are easy to handle and portable. Most of the projects are hand appliquéd with a blanket stitch or fancy stitch variations. Take time to look at the diagrams and directions on page 19 to refresh your memory or to learn a new way to do this time-honored stitch.

See Machine Appliqué (page 20) for instructions on adapting projects for machine appliqué. Wait to sew the

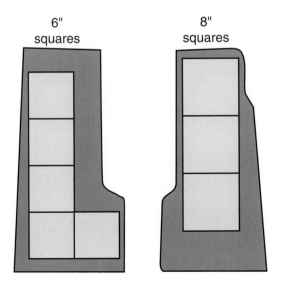
6"
squares
8"
squares

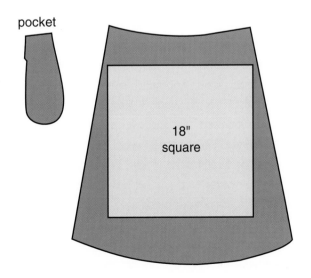
pocket
18"
square

Figure 3. Cutting blocks from skirts.

blocks together until after the appliqué is complete whether you are stitching by hand or machine.

Wool appliqué shapes. Keep the shapes simple for quick and easy appliqué with a folk-art look. Simple shapes are easy for beginners. A wide variety of designs are included in the project and pattern sections. Other excellent sources for designs include cookie cutters and coloring books, or try your hand at cutting free-form shapes. When designing an original work, remember, the appliqué needs to be suited to the blanket stitch. In general, avoid points that are too sharp and very small pieces (Figure 4).

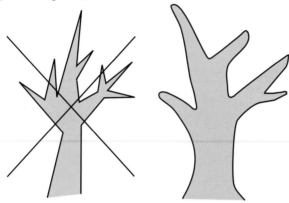

Figure 4. In designing appliqué, avoid sharp points.

Templates. Use freezer paper for appliqué templates. It is transparent enough to trace a design, and it is easy to draw on as well. Once you have traced your design on the dull side of the freezer paper, iron the tracing directly on the wool and cut the template and the wool piece together. If you would prefer not to cut paper with your fabric scissors, cut the paper first with paper-cutting scissors, press the shape on the wool, and then cut out the wool shape. There is no need to trace around the template directly on the wool. A single freezer-paper template can be used over and over again until it gets too fuzzy to stick. Because most wool fabric does not have a right or wrong side, simply turn the appliqué piece over to reverse a directional design. Remove the paper before stitching your piece.

If you are fusing the appliqué, forego the freezer paper and trace your designs directly on the fusing web. Follow the directions on the fusing web. When fusing

your designs, you will need to pay attention to the direction you want the finished appliqué to face since you will not be able to turn these pieces over to change the direction.

If the appliqué fabric frays as you remove the freezer paper, now is the time to make a decision about using that piece. You may continue and just handle the piece very gently as you work. If you are hand blanket stitching the appliqué, you can gently pull the frays in with your stitch. You can use a fray sealant. You may want to take a little deeper 'bite' as you stitch by hand or machine. Another option if the fraying seems like too much trouble is to pitch it and choose another piece of wool.

Placing appliqués. If you are making a quilt, center the appliqué shapes on each background square. If you are

Figure 5. For pillows, place appliqué pieces toward the center of the pillow.

Heart-Felt Wool Appliqué — Lorinda Lie

making a pillow top with more than one appliquéd block, move the shapes slightly closer to the center of the pillow top. Consider placing a circle, button, or other appliqué shape in the center of the pillow to avoid having a big empty space. The puffiness of the pillow will only accentuate an empty spot (Figure 5).

Even felted wool has some stretch and give to it. While it is not particularly fragile, it does require gentle handling to keep from pulling it out of shape or overworking the edges. When placing appliqués on a background, three or four pins should be sufficient to hold most pieces. Basting is recommended for larger or more complex shapes, such as those for the TULIP GARDEN wallhanging (page 60), and Hawaiian cutwork (page 50).

Pin from the back of the block to keep the thread from getting caught on the pins as you stitch. Even easier, staple the shapes in place. Use a regular stapler and quality staples. The weave of the wool will let the staples slip between the threads without damaging them.

Hand appliqué

Threads and needles. Several threads lend themselves to blanket-stitch appliqué. The easiest to use and the most economical is regular embroidery floss. Use a quality brand. Cut about a 24" piece of floss. Separate it into strands and use at least three strands together for wool appliqué. If you prefer a thicker outline or you are using heavier weight wool, more strands may be necessary to make an attractive edge. Do not double the thread.

Size 5 perle cotton has a sheen to it, is a little heavier than embroidery floss, and makes a nice edge. Yarn is challenging to use. It tends to fray as you sew and is not recommended if a crisp look is desired.

Thread that matches the appliqué piece will disguise your stitches and may be the most comfortable for a beginner. Contrasting thread is more visible and becomes a stronger design element. This visibility makes the thread easier to see your stitches as you work. Choose an appropriate needle for the thread. An embroidery needle has a large eye to accommodate the

floss and a sharp point to penetrate the fabric. The needle needs to be large enough to make a hole in the fabric for the thread to glide through. If you have to tug the needle with each stitch, try a larger needle. Remember, the smaller the number, the larger the needle. A size 7 embroidery needle is a good size for three strands of regular floss. Try a size 5 needle with size 5 perle cotton.

Hand blanket stitch. Knot your thread. Start sewing on a fairly straight edge away from a point or corner. Come up from the back in the background fabric, next to the edge of the appliqué (Figure 6). Take your first stitch right where your needle came up. It will have bite but no distance. Hold the block so you are working along the top edge of the appliqué. The direction of your stitches will be to the right if you are right-handed and to the left if you are left-handed. You will always be moving the needle directly away from your body. It may feel awkward at first, but the needle will always come up inside the loop, and your stitches will be even and square. Turn the block as you work (Figure 7, page 16).

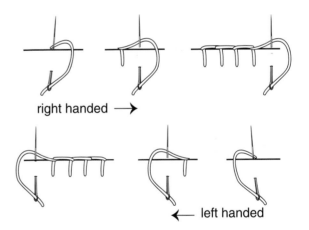

right handed →

← left handed

Figure 6. Basic blanket stitch.

Stitch Tension

If your piece isn't lying flat or it appears pinched and puckered, you are pulling the thread too tight. As you make each stitch, pull the thread just until the stitch is square. If the appliqué is loose, you are not pulling the thread taut enough; pull it just a bit tighter. If the appliqué is completely loose, you are not catching the bottom fabric in your stitch. Try taking a slightly bigger bite.

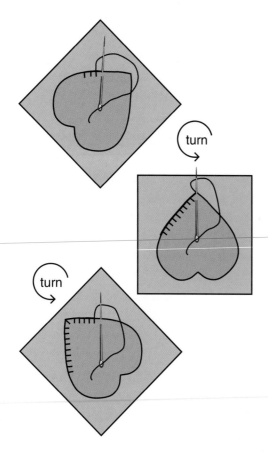

Figure 7. Start on a straight edge, stitch the point, and turn to the next side.

To make a basic blanket stitch, aim for the distance to equal the bite for a consistent stitch. A good stitch is ⅛" – ³⁄₁₆" in bite and distance. Some of the primitive stitches, while popular, are too big to be sturdy over time. Most of the projects in this book are meant to be used. These utility quilts not only have to stand up to heavy use but also to occasional washing.

Points and corners require special treatment. While your overall goal is an even distance between stitches, as you approach corners and points, this may not always be possible. When you approach a corner or point, think of an imaginary line running through the center. Reduce the distance between stitches as you approach. In the case of points, the bite will need to be reduced as well so you don't stitch over the imaginary line. Consistency is the key. Whatever changes are made to stitch bite and distance on one side of a corner or point should be mirrored on the other side (Figure 8).

For any point that is 90 degrees or sharper, you will need an extra stitch to anchor the point. Failure to do so will cause the stitch to float; that is, it will be loose and the point will not be sharp and crisp. Take the first stitch right

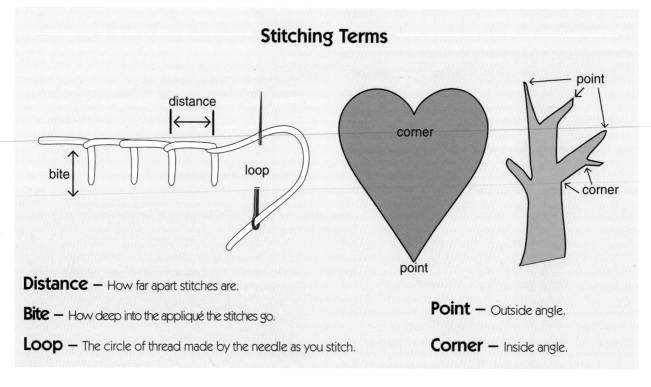

Stitching Terms

distance

bite

loop

corner

point

point

corner

Distance – How far apart stitches are.

Bite – How deep into the appliqué the stitches go.

Loop – The circle of thread made by the needle as you stitch.

Point – Outside angle.

Corner – Inside angle.

Heart-Felt Wool Appliqué — Lorinda Lie

Hand Blanket Stitch

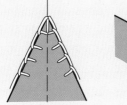
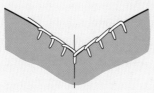
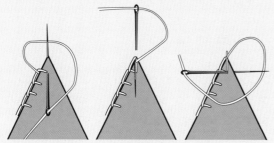

Figure 8. Stitches should mirror each other in distance and bite on both sides of an imaginary center line.

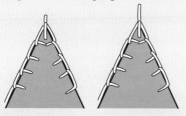

Figure 9. Steps in anchoring a point.

Figure 10. You can use a short or elongated anchoring stitch.

Figure 11. Soften appearance by rounding off points.

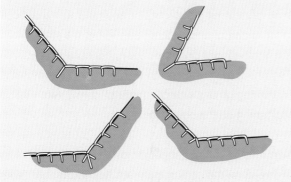

Figure 12. Options for handling corners.

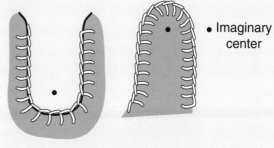

• Imaginary center

Figure 13. For curves, bites should be like spokes in a wheel.

Figure 14. For very small circles, use the same hole in the center for all the stitches.

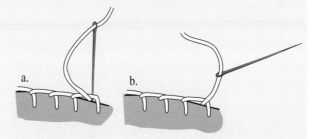

Figure 15. a. Ending thread. b. Joining thread. New thread should come up inside the last loop.

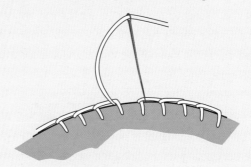

Figure 16. Connecting stitch.

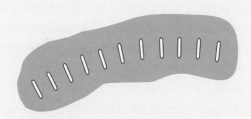

Figure 17. Blanket stitch as seen from the back.

on the imaginary line bisecting the point. Instead of continuing with the next stitch, anchor the first stitch by bringing the needle to the back. Pull the thread tight and come up inside the first stitch as shown in Figure 9, page 17.

For very sharp crisp points, elongate the extra stitch into the background fabric (Figure 10). This tricks the eye into seeing a sharper point. Incidentally, this trick works well on any kind of appliqué and is ideal for leaves.

If you would prefer a softer look, you can round points slightly. The overall shape of the piece will not be affected (Figure 11).

Corners can be handled several ways. No matter what way you choose, make all the corners on a single piece the same for a consistent and polished finish. See Figure 12 for different stitching options.

Small circles and tight curves also require special handling. In a tight curve, the bite should always be in alignment with the center of an imaginary circle like a spoke on a wheel (Figure 13). For very small circles, reuse the same hole in the center of the circle (Figure 14).

To end a piece of thread, finish a complete stitch, then bring the thread to the back to anchor the last stitch. Take a couple of stitches in the back only. Begin a new thread inside the loop of the last stitch for a continuous look (Figure 15).

To finish the appliqué, gradually make the last few stitches a bit larger or smaller as needed to end with a complete connecting stitch. Bring the needle down inside the loop of the beginning stitch (Figure 16).

Anchor the thread on the back with a few stitches taken in place. In a well-done piece of blanket-stitched appliqué, the casual viewer will not be able to see where the thread began or ended.

While you see a continuous line of thread on the front of your blanket-stitched appliqué piece, the back looks like unconnected parallel lines. These should be even in length and distance apart (Figure 17).

Fancy hand blanket stitches. These stitches are variations of the basic blanket stitch. They are all made with a loop of thread that is anchored in place. They vary in bite, distance, and needle angle. As you work with these stitches, you may create variations of your own. Don't forget, the purpose of the stitch is to anchor the appliqué in place and to finish the edge, as well as to add interest. All diagrams are for right-handed stitches. Reverse direction if you are left-handed.

Embroidery stitches can be used to add interest to your piece (Photo 1). For sources of embroidery stitches, check the bibliography on page 110.

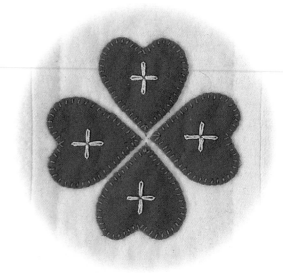

Photo 1: Close-up of QUILTER'S CROSSWORD (page 70) shows basic blanket stitch and lazy daisy stitch.

Short of drawing the stitches on each piece, it is difficult to tell ahead of time where you will be in a stitch when you get to a point or corner. The rule is consistency. Even if you have to vary the stitch slightly, try to mirror what is happening on one side of a point or corner with what is happening on the other side.

Add interest to your appliqué by using multiple colors of thread on the combination stitches. Experiment with contrasting and variegated threads.

Heart-Felt Wool Appliqué — Lorinda Lie

Fancy Hand Blanket Stitches

Distance and Bite Variations

3-3-3

long-short

2-2-2

short-long-short

Angle Variations

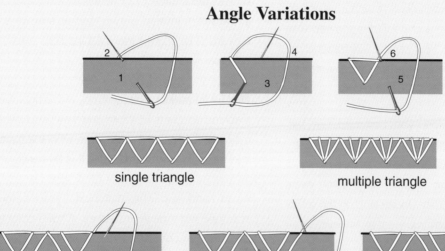

single triangle

multiple triangle

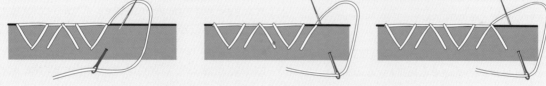

Combination and Other Stitches

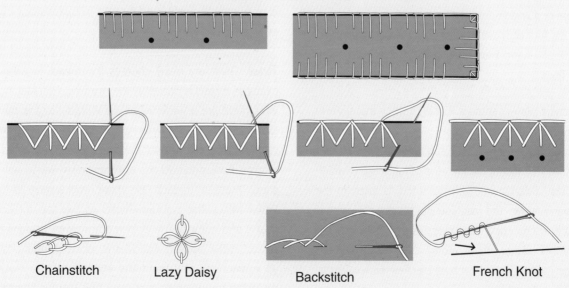

Chainstitch   Lazy Daisy   Backstitch   French Knot

Machine appliqué

While I find hand appliquéing relaxing and portable, I know some of you probably prefer the speed of machine appliqué. With practice, the look is more polished but still charming. Follow the instructions here, and for the machine you are using, to adapt any of the projects in this book for machine appliqué.

It's best to follow the specifications given for your machine and practice on scraps of fabric before beginning any project. Try different threads, stabilizers, stitches, and stitch settings to find the ones that work best for you and your machine. Experimenting with a variety of machines, settings, threads, and stabilizers showed that most worked equally well. Your choice will depend on your machine and your preferences for preparation and cleanup.

Machine blanket stitch. Before you begin to use the machine blanket stitch with your wool, it is helpful to understand the properties unique to both hand and machine stitches. They are not the same stitch even though they mimic each other. Understanding the stitch will help you create the look you want to achieve.

The hand blanket stitch is a looped stitch that floats along the edge of the appliqué. Ideally, you want to use a thread that will come close to covering the edge of the appliqué. That's why we used three strands of embroidery floss or #5 perle cotton. On heavier pieces of wool, it may take four or six strands of floss to cover the edge. The back of a hand blanket stitch is a series of straight, parallel lines.

The machine blanket stitch is a straight stitch that sews in two directions, forward and sideways. It takes a stitch into the appliqué, which is the stitch width, or what was called bite in hand appliqué. The stitch length, which was called distance in the hand stitch, is taken in the background fabric. The machine stitch along the edge is by nature less conspicuous because it is taken in the background rather than along the edge of the appliqué. The back of a machine blanket stitch will mirror the front if the tension is adjusted correctly.

Because the stitch length is taken in the background fabric instead of on the edge, the machine blanket stitch is not suitable as a finish on outside edges. Practice on your machine so you know where the stitch starts and stops and what constitutes a stitch on your machine. Practice will also get you used to the rhythm of the stitch, rounding curves, and making corners and points, before beginning your project.

Depending on your machine, you can make the thread "thicker" to look more like embroidery floss in several ways: (1) Use double thread; (2) Use a heavier thread, such as jeans thread; (3) Increase the number of repeats in the stitch. Instead of two stitches sideways and one forward ($2/1$), change the machine setting to $4/3$ or $6/5$ if your machine has this capability.

Wool for the machine. Choose wool with a tight weave. The machine needle is less forgiving than hand stitching and may fray the edges. It is harder to work the frayed edges into the stitch by machine than it is by hand.

As in hand appliqué, matching thread colors to the appliqué will hide your stitches. A solid color appliqué piece and a contrasting thread color will show off stitches the most. For large machine projects, you may want to use only one color of thread for all the appliqué pieces, as in the BUTTON QUILT (page 36) or TWO CATS IN A POSY PATCH Pillow (page 66). One color of thread creates an old-time look, and it saves frequent stopping to change thread color.

Thread. There are many choices for thread. Regular all-purpose thread is probably the most economical; however, there are a wide variety of threads on the market designed to be used with newer machines. Experiment with cotton, rayon, and metallic threads for different effects. Cotton thread has a flatter finish. Rayon will be shiny. Metallic threads are more challenging to use. Either match the bobbin thread to the top thread in brand and color or use cotton embroidery and basting thread in the bobbin. Follow the recommendations for your machine. You want the strength of the bobbin thread to be the same or weaker than the top thread.

If you are using double thread, try two different colors for an interesting effect. Double thread will give you a thicker stitch, more like the hand appliqué stitch. See THOSE CRAZY BLUES Vest (page 38).

Stabilizers. Machine appliqué and embroidery require a stabilizer to help the fabric hold its shape as you sew. Without a stabilizer, the stitches may pull or curl the edge of appliqué or stretch the wool. There are several basic ways to stabilize wool. Use a tear-away stabilizer underneath the block. Fuse the appliqué piece to the block before embroidering. Stabilize a muslin base with heavy-duty spray starch, then place it under the wool background square before appliquéing. Saturate the wool and wool appliqué pieces with heavy-duty spray starch and embroider. Some people have good luck using doctors' paper or freezer paper underneath the background block.

Use one or two layers of tear-away stabilizer depending on the strength needed. If you are using paper, one layer should be sufficient. The drawback to using tear-away stabilizers or paper is that they need to be removed from the back. This takes time and can be tedious work. Make sure the stitch isn't stretched or distorted when you tear the stabilizer away. Some snippets of these stabilizers may be caught in the threads and show. This is not an issue with quilted items where the back will be covered by batting and backing. The advantage of tear-away stabilizers is that your appliquéd block will be softer and easier to quilt. As always, experiment with a variety of brands and weights until you find a product you like. You will need to baste or pin your appliqué pieces in place before beginning the embroidery.

If you choose to fuse the appliqué, there is a wide variety of fusing webs on the market. Use the lightest one that will do the job. The drawback to fusing webs is that they make the appliqué piece somewhat stiff. For the most part, this is not a problem unless you want to hand quilt through the appliqué. The advantage is that it makes the piece easiest to appliqué because the wool will not stretch or shift as you appliqué it and no pins are necessary.

To use a muslin base as a stabilizer, saturate the muslin with heavy-duty spray starch. You may want to do this a couple of times to get a good, stiff base. Heavy-duty starch works better than regular. The starch will rinse out of the project after it is finished. This method works best in an unquilted projects like THOSE CRAZY BLUES Vest (page 38) or on a project that is machine quilted because the extra layer of fabric will make hand quilting more difficult.

Machine settings. If you have a setting for an automatic stop at the end of a stitch, use this on your practice piece to help you understand the stitch on your machine. You need to know where the stitch starts and stops and which direction it will sew first. This is particularly important on points and corners.

Use the needle-down setting. This feature will help you control your stitches on points, corners, and curves so that your stitches will be square.

Find a stitch setting that is comfortable for you. You need a wide enough stitch to secure the wool appliqué in place. Remember, wool is a much larger fiber than cotton, and consequently it is a much looser weave. Be sure you catch several threads in the blanket stitch. You want this stitch to show. Keep the stitch length and width close together for square stitches.

If you are new to machine blanket stitch appliqué, begin practicing with a fairly small stitch. The smaller stitch will be easier to control while sewing around sharp points, corners, and curves. Gradually work toward a larger stitch as you learn to control the needle and stitch settings on points and corners. A medium to large stitch will look most like handwork.

Follow the automatic tension settings on your machine or use a lower tension. Try automatic settings first for heavy woven fabric or heavy stretch fabric. You will need to do some trial runs to find the best settings for you and your machine. Reduce the pressure slightly on the presser foot if you can.

Presser feet. The best foot for machine blanket stitching is an open-toed embroidery foot. This foot is designed to give you the best view of what you are stitching. It will be particularly helpful for points and corners and for ending a closed appliqué piece. The next best foot is a see-through plastic one. It will give you a somewhat better view of what you are stitching than a regular metal foot.

Machine stitching. Pin, baste or fuse your appliqué pieces in place. Start stitching on a long side, away from points and corners so you have control of your stitch before working on more challenging spots.

Turn your appliqué piece clockwise as you work along the right-hand side of the appliqué piece. You may need to use the side-to-side mirror image if your machine has this feature.

For beginners in machine appliqué, gently rounded points are recommended. You still may need to shorten the stitch width and length some, but you have a little more leeway in rounding the points than you would with very sharp points.

If you choose to keep sharp points, look again at the diagrams for hand-stitched points and corners (page 16). The machine blanket stitch works the same way. Picture an imaginary line running through the point or corner. Mirror the two sides. You may need to adjust both stitch length and width as you approach and round points and corners. If you want the look of an elongated point, reset your machine and take a straight stitch at the point. It leads your eye to see the points as very sharp.

Stitch slowly for best control. Use a stiletto or metal hem gauge to guide your work and ease the wool under the foot. As you stitch curves, turn your piece frequently so the stitch width is always perpendicular to the edge of the appliqué as in spokes on a wheel. If you work too quickly, you may have a slanted stitch rather than a nice square stitch.

To end stitching, adjust the length of the last few stitches so the piece ends where it started, with a smooth continuous look, just as in hand stitching.

Quilt Assembly

All the projects in this book allow for a scant ½" seam allowance unless otherwise noted. When you are ready to join your blocks, pin them right sides together with three or four pins. Use a walking foot or even-feed foot on your sewing machine. If you don't have one, most sewing-machine or fabric stores can order one for you. If you have an adjustable presser foot, reduce the pressure on the foot so the wool doesn't get pushed or stretched as you sew it. You want both pieces of wool to pass under the needle evenly and freely.

Press the seam allowances open to reduce overall bulk and bulk at seam intersections. Using steam alone or in combination with a clapper will help set the seam allowances open. Now that your project is appliquéd and pieced, it is time to think about quilting and finishing options.

Batting. A good choice for wool quilts is a lightweight, bonded polyester batting, such as Thermore™, which is used in clothing. It is very thin, 3
easy to quilt, and guaranteed not to beard. It has a nice drape and adds a bit of body to the quilt without making it overly heavy. Polyester battings that are not bonded are likely to beard when used with wool, a problem especially noticeable on dark colors.

The natural-fiber battings, cotton and wool, also work well and do not beard. They will add warmth and weight to your quilt. A wool batting will add the most loft. It is more expensive, but don't ignore wool as a viable option. Besides being a warm batting, it breathes so you won't feel as sweaty as with polyester batting. It is also safer for kids because of its flame-resistant properties. Leaving out the batting entirely or using flannel for the middle layer of the sandwich can also be effective in creating a quilt that breathes but is not too heavy.

Backing. Choose a backing with warmth in mind. Flannel and cotton are both suitable. Flannel will feel warmer than cotton and it is somewhat heavier. It has a cozy feel for a country quilt. On the down side, flannel tends to stretch more than cotton, and it may be slightly more

Heart-Felt Wool Appliqué — Lorinda Lie

difficult to quilt. Quilter's cotton is the lightest weight backing and it is less stretchy. It will lend stability, making it easier to quilt. It will give the back of the quilt a cooler feel.

Backing sometimes needs to be pieced. Cut the yardage in half from selvedge to selvedge. Trim off the selvedges and sew panels together on one long edge (Figure 18).

Quilting

Wool quilts may be either hand or machine quilted with relative ease. For the simplest design, quilt around each appliqué and ½" to ¾" on both sides of each seam allowance. Remember that the seam allowances have been pressed open so do not quilt in the ditch.

Marking. Wool quilts are more difficult to mark than cotton, particularly dark quilts. Mark light-colored wools by using a turquoise washout marker. It will mark easily and should wash out in cold water. Be sure to test any marker on a piece of your wool to make sure it will wash out. Darker wool can be marked with a soapstone pencil, chalk marker, white wax marking pencil, or chalk pouncing tool. Because these materials may brush off, mark the quilt a small section at a time, spray with hair spray, then quilt. Masking tape is a helpful guide for straight lines.

Hand quilting. Don't be afraid to hand quilt your wool quilt. You will find your needle slips through wool like going through butter. These are folk quilts, utility quilts. You do not want to use your finest stitch on these projects; in fact too fine a stitch will slip between the threads of the wool and be lost or appear as a skipped stitch. You also want to avoid "toe-hooker" loops that won't stand up to repeated use. Use your usual size of quilting needle.

Machine quilting. Be sure to support the weight of the quilt as you quilt it. Wool quilts are heavy. Use a walking foot for straight rows. Use a darning or embroidery foot for free-motion quilting. These feet have a spring that lifts the foot so you can move the fabric in any direction. They are used with the feed dogs dropped or covered. Reduce pressure on your presser foot so the wool glides

under the foot evenly. Use a moderate-sized stitch. Gently ease the quilt under the presser foot, making sure the weight of the quilt is supported everywhere so it doesn't stretch.

Finishing

Binding edges. The quilts in the projects generally have a wider binding than cotton quilts, but there are still several different methods to choose from.

Straight-grain binding. For ½" finished binding, cut straight-grain cotton strips 3" wide on the cross grain. The strips are sewn on the bias, and the seam allowances are pressed open. After the strips have been sewn together to make one long continuous strip, fold the strip in half, wrong sides together. Sew the binding on the right side of the quilt by machine, with a ½" seam allowance. Miter the corners. Tack the binding on the back of the quilt by hand. Tack the miters in the corners.

Bias binding. For a quilt with rounded corners, like the FAN DANCE, page 54, or for bias-bound clothing, cut the binding on the bias so it will go around the curves smoothly. Cut it 3" wide. Piece as necessary on the diagonal. Fold the long continuous strip in half, wrong sides together, and sew on the quilt as for straight-grain binding.

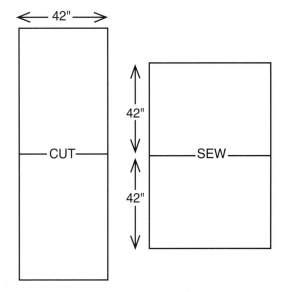

Figure 18. Cut yardage in half, turn panels a quarter turn, and join.

Stuffed Binding

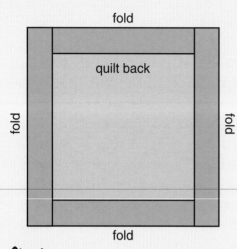

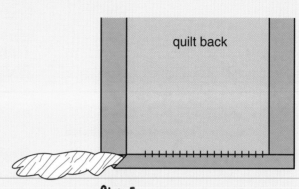

Step 1.
Sew folded binding strips to top, bottom, and sides of quilt.

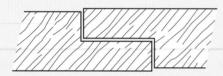

Step 2.
Trim batting ends to interlock them.

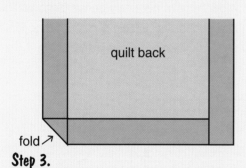

fold ↗

Step 3.
Fold corner.

Step 5.
Fold binding over batting and stitch to corner.

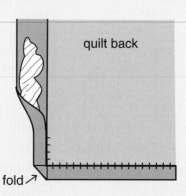

Step 6.
Fold binding over batting and stitch.

Step 4.
Fold binding over batting and tack in place.

fold ↗

Step 7.
Fold corner again and stitch it closed.

Stuffed binding. This special binding is easy to do and makes a great finish on almost any quilt or pillow. Kids love it because it makes a nice handle. Because it finishes approximately 1" wide, it can also be an important design element.

Cut two 5" cross-grain strips that are as long as the unfinished width of the quilt top. Fold them in half, wrong sides together. Using a ½" seam allowance, sew the strips to the quilt top and bottom, on the front of the quilt. Press the allowances toward the binding (page 24, Step 1).

Cut four more 5" cross-grain strips. Piece them to make two strips the length of your quilt top plus 9", the combined widths of the sewn binding strips on the top and bottom. A diagonal seam is the least obtrusive. Press the strips in half lengthwise, wrong sides together, and sew them in place on each side of the quilt. Press the seam allowances toward the binding. Ignore the raw edges for now.

Cut strips of batting 4"–6" wide, depending on the puffiness of the batting. Cut wider strips if the batting is thin. Polyester batting can be used in the stuffed binding, which is a great way to use all those leftover pieces from other projects. To join batting pieces, cut the ends and butt them together as shown in Step 2.

Start in the center of one side (Step 3). Scrunch the batting together and lay it on the binding. Fold the binding

over the batting and tack the binding in place by hand on the back of the quilt.

Follow the diagrams in Steps 5–6, to make neat, smooth corners. Continue stuffing and stitching, adding new pieces of batting as needed.

Finishing a pillow. The pillows in the project section all have lapped cotton backs. Various edge treatments can be used successfully with wool pillows.

Lapped back. For a 14" pillow, cut two cotton back pieces 15" by 11". (See individual pattern directions for other pillow sizes.) Hem one 15" edge on each rectangle by pressing under ¼" along the edge. Press under another ¾" on the same edge and sew the hem in place (Figure 19). Overlap the hemmed edges to make 15" square with raw edges on all outside edges. Finish according to individual pattern directions.

Turned edges. Pillows can be made without any special edge treatment. Layer the quilted or unquilted pillow top and lapped back right sides together. Stitch around outside edge with a ½" seam allowance. Trim the excess fabric from the corners and turn pillow right side out. Stuff the pillow with a purchased pillow form.

Bound edges. For bound pillows, layer finished quilted or unquilted pillow top and lapped back wrong sides together. Baste around the edges with a walking foot and long machine stitches. Bind the raw edges with straight-grain or stuffed binding, described on page 24.

Ruffled edges. Cut 5" strips of cotton fabric on the cross grain. You will need to piece a length 2½ times the perimeter of the pillow. Piece the strips together, with a diagonal seam, to make one long, continuous strip. Press seam allowances open. Connect the two ends to make a circle.

Press the strip in half, wrong sides together. Divide the circle into eighths and mark the divisions. To gather the circle into a ruffle, use a medium-sized zigzag stitch

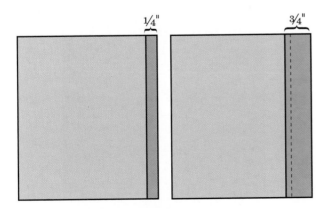

Figure 19. Turn under ¼" and press. Turn again ¾" and press. Stitch close to the edge as shown.

Heart-Felt Wool Appliqué — Lorinda Lie

over #8 perle cotton or buttonhole twist as shown in Figure 20. If you keep a little bit of tension on the perle cotton or button-hole twist, it will gather fairly uniformly behind the presser foot.

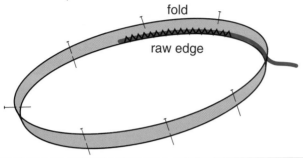

Figure 20. Use zigzag stitch to sew perle cotton or button hole twist approximately ¼" from the raw edge.

Pin the ruffle in place on the front of the pillow with the raw edges together. Match the division marks with the corners and the center of each side of the pillow. Draw up the perle cotton or button hole twist until the ruffle fits. Baste in place (Figure 21). Place top and back sections with raw edges and right sides together. Sew around the outside edge of the pillow (½" seam allowance), being careful not to catch the ruffle at the corners. Zigzag raw edges together. Turn the pillow right side out and stuff it with a purchased pillow form.

Unquilted pillows with tongues. Tongues are one of the traditional finishes our foremothers used for wool penny rugs. The rugs, actually table mats, were made of layers

of circles that were blanket stitched to a foundation. The wool tongues create a giant fringe around the outside edge. A pattern has been included for a 1½" tongue to use for your pillows (page 90). Each tongue is a single layer of wool, which is blanket stitched around the curved edge (Figure 22). A machine blanket stitch is not suitable for tongues.

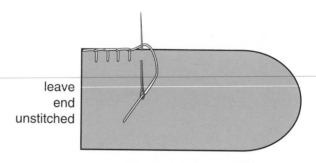

Figure 22. Blanket stitch around the outside edges of each tongue.

How you attach the tongues to your pillow depends on whether it is quilted or not. For an unquilted pillow top, space the tongues evenly on the right side, along the edges, ending ⅝" from the corners (Figure 23).

Baste the tongues in place. Layer the pillow top and lapped back, right sides together, aligning the raw edges with the sides of the pillow top. Sew around the pillow with a ½" seam allowance. Turn the pillow right side out. Press the tongues to the outside and press the edges of the pillow by using a clapper, if you have one.

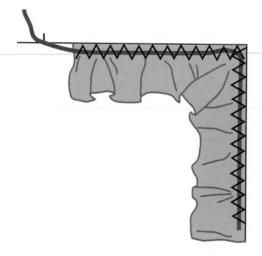

Figure 21. Use the perle cotton to draw up the ruffle.

Figure 23. Space tongues on the right side of an unquilted pillow top and baste.

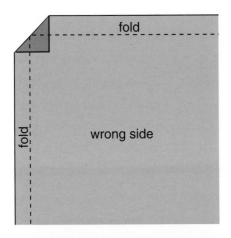

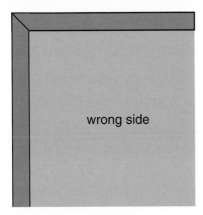

Figure 24. To prepare the backing for a quilted pillow top, fold the corners and press a **½"** seam allowance to the wrong side.

Quilted pillows with tongues. While penny rugs were traditionally not quilted, quilting does add extra dimension to a piece. Use the following directions to achieve a nice finished edge for a quilted pillow with tongues. It requires a few extra steps to reduce the bulk at the seam and hide the batting.

Choose a fabric for the pillow-top backing that will blend with the top and the tongues because the backing may show. Cut the backing to the finished size of the pillow plus 1" for seam allowances. Press a ½" seam allowance to the wrong side all around, mitering the corners (Figure 24).

Cut the batting the finished size and center it on the backing. Place the folded edge over the batting. Trim the pillow top to the finished size. Place the top on the batting and backing, wrong sides together, matching edges and corners. Pin in place and blanket stitch around the edge of the pillow top with a stitch width and bite of about ³⁄₁₆" (Figure 25). Quilt the pillow top following individual pattern directions.

Make pieces for a lapped pillow back as described on page 25. Overlap the two rectangles to make a square the size of your pillow, including seam allowances. For most of the pillows shown, this will be 15". Lay tongues on the right side of the fabric around all sides of the lapped back, ending ⅝" from the corners (Figure 26). Baste.

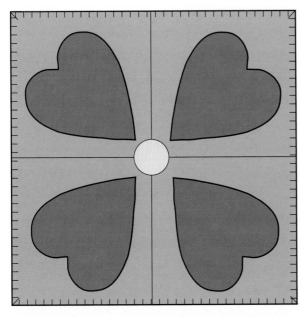

Figure 25. Blanket stitch pillow and backing together.

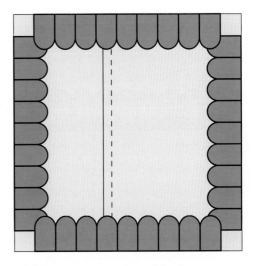

Figure 26. Lay tongues on lapped back.

Heart-Felt Wool Appliqué — Lorinda Lie

Sew tongues to lapped back with a ½" seam allowance. Turn the lapped back to the wrong side. Fold corners in, as before (Figure 27). Press tongues to the outside. If desired, lay corner tongues in place on the wrong side (Figure 28). Pin in place and stitch around back just inside stitching line, anchoring corner tongues. Slip-stitch quilted pillow top together with the lapped back and tongues. Stuff with a pillow form.

Care of finished projects. Quilts, wallhangings, pillows, and vests made from felted wool may be laundered. Be sure to use cold water, mild soap, and a short, very gentle cycle with little or no agitation. Spin out as much water as you can and lay the piece flat to dry. Avoid hot water and strong agitation, which cause shrinkage. Remember, that's how we felted the wool. For quilts with wool batting, follow the recommendations on the package.

As with any wool garment, store your wool quilts clean. Food spills attract bugs. Cedar chests are ideal for long-term storage (See also Storing Wool Fabric, page 12).

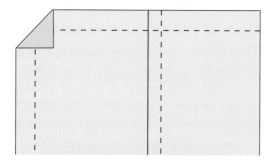

Figure 27. Fold corners to the wrong side.

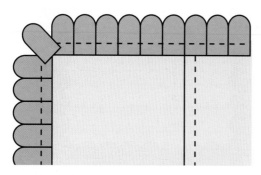

Figure 28. Press tongues to the outside and lay corner tongues in place.

Collecting Wool

Button Quilt, page 36
Grays and camels are some of the easiest and most available colors to collect or purchase. The quilt would be pretty in any color family or it can be a scrap quilt. The quilt pictured has about a dozen different wool fabrics in it.

Falling Leaves Quilt, page 44
Don't limit yourself to skirts for this quilt. Some of the richest browns and dusky greens come from men's trousers. You can also use suit jackets.

Primary Bulbs and Warm Welcome Wallhanging, pages 50 and 53
The larger block size in these wallhangings requires greater care in choosing garments. Look for skirts in larger sizes or gathered skirts that will yield at least a 20" unblemished square. Remember that you have to allow for shrinkage during felting. Make sure a cut dart, pocket opening, or open pleat doesn't mar the square area. A straight seam is no problem.

Fan Dance Quilt, page 54
Ask in menswear departments for discontinued suiting swatches. Many are just the right size for the fans. If the samples are glued to cards, try to remove as much paper as possible. If a little remains, you can work around it as you piece. Trimmings from men's pant hems are another good source. Ask a tailor or person who does alterations. If you need to purchase garments or wool for this project, look for worsted weight wool and men's trousers.

Tulip Garden Wallhanging, page 60
Because of the shapes and sizes needed, purchase this yardage new. It may be as easy or economical to purchase small squares at a quilt shop.

Springtime Vest, page 64
Look for skirts in spring colors that go together. The appliqué will tie the vest together. Another option would be to purchase wool or use a combination of new and used wool.

Part Two: Projects

Detail from PRIMARY BULBS

Scrappy Projects:
Pot Luck Scrap Quilt

FRED'S QUILT, designed, hand appliquéd, and hand quilted by Jo Fifield. Most of the letters in the quilt are randomly placed, but can you find the five vowels and a name?

Pot Luck Scrap Quilt

Beginner level
49" x 77" topper or nap quilt
7" finished blocks

This scrap quilt is an ideal project for anyone beginning to work with wool. You can start soon as you have five or six wool pieces.

My long-time quilting partner, Jo Fifield, designed the alphabet and made this quilt for her husband, Fred. Once they discover the unique properties and warmth of wool, every family member will be wanting their own. Except for the holly and the letters spelling "Fred," the appliqué designs are placed on every other block.

Variations

• *Use a theme, such as flowers or a holiday. Wool would be perfect for a special Christmas quilt. Use your favorite Christmas cookie cutters for appliqué templates.*
• *Make this a sampler quilt and experiment with different techniques, such as rounded and sharp points, contrasting and matching thread, embroidery floss and perle cotton, basic and fancy stitches, machine and hand appliqué.*

Quilt Assembly

1 Prepare wool: If you are new to wool quilts, be sure to read Learning the Basics, pages 8–28, for directions on felting wool, and tips for how to work with it by hand or machine.

2 Cut squares: You will need 77 squares, 8" x 8", of felted wool. Begin by cutting two or three squares from each piece of wool. Cut more squares as you collect more wool. Use leftover scraps for appliqués.

3 Cut appliqués: You will need to create approximately 39 shapes or choose shapes for the blocks from the pattern section. Trace the shapes on the dull side of freezer paper and cut them out to use as templates. Iron the templates on the appropriate wool fabrics. Cut the wool appliqué pieces, gently rounding sharp points. To make a reversed shape, just turn wool piece over.

4 Appliqué blocks: Pin the wool appliqué shapes to the blocks and blanket-stitch them in place with three strands of embroidery floss. Practice making your stitches even and consistent.

5 Join blocks: Use a ½" seam allowance to sew the blocks together in two- and four-block units, then in quarter sections. Place a walking foot on your sewing machine and reduce the pressure on the presser foot. Sew the sections together to complete the top. Press all the seam allowances open.

6 Layer quilt: Trim the selvages from the backing fabric and cut backing into two 1½-yard pieces. Turn them and resew as shown in the Figure 28 (page 28). The backing will measure approximately 54" by 84". Layer the backing, batting, and top; baste.

7 Quilt layers: Hand quilt ¾" from the seam line around each block. For a perfect quilting guide, use ¾" masking tape. Hand-quilt around the appliqué shapes. Quilt a 3" to 4" square in the center of the blank squares by using masking tape as a guide.

8 Finish quilt: Cut 3" strips of cotton for straight-grain binding. Piece the strips together, end to end, on the diagonal. Fold the pieced strip in half lengthwise, wrong sides together, and sew the strip to the right side of the quilt with a ½" seam allowance. Miter the corners. Hand-stitch the binding to the back of the quilt and tack the miters closed. Add a label and enjoy.

Materials (see Collecting Wool, page 35)

• 4½ yds. wool – variety of wool skirts or fabric in solids and plaids
• 3 yds. cotton for backing
• ⅞ yds. cotton for straight-grain binding
• Assorted colors of embroidery floss
• Batting (Thermore, page 22)
• Freezer paper

Patterns

Large Holly Leaf and Berry, Watering Can, page 75
Tree, Dove, Apple, page 76
Maple Leaf, Hearts, page 79
Alphabet and Numbers, pages 101–110

Scrappy Projects:
Folk Leaves and Penny Circles Pillow

by Barbara Scoggins

Materials

- Four 8" squares felted wool: two squares color A, one square color B, and one plaid square
- Felted wool scraps for appliqué
- ½ yd. cotton for lapped pillow back
- Assorted colors of embroidery floss
- Freezer paper
- 13" pillow form. Make your own or use a 14" form for a very full pillow.

Patterns

Folk Leaf, page 81
Penny Circle Set B, page 93

Folk Leaves and Penny Circles Pillow

Beginner level
13" pillow

Have leftover squares from the POT LUCK quilt? This pillow starts with four 8" squares: two of color A, one of color B, and one plaid square.

Pillow Assembly

1 Prepare wool: If you are new to wool quilts, be sure to read Learning the Basics, pages 8–28, for directions on felting wool, and tips for how to work with it by hand or machine.

2 Cut background: Cut the two color-A squares in half. Cut the color-B square in fourths (Figure 29). Leave the plaid square whole.

3 Join background pieces: Follow Figure 30 to sew the pieces together with a ½" seam allowance before appliquéing. Press all seam allowances open to reduce bulk at the seam intersections.

4 Cut appliqués: Trace the designs for the folk leaf and penny circles, set B, on freezer paper. Cut and iron them on wool scraps. Cut the appliqués and arrange them as shown in the photograph, or as desired, and blanket-stitch them in place.

5 Finish pillow: Follow the basic directions on page 23 to finish the pillow, which is not layered or quilted. Cut rectangles for a lapped back 10½" by 14". The pillow is turned, with no binding or other edge finish.

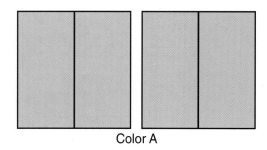

Color A

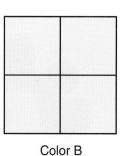

Color B

Figure 29. Cut color A in half and color B in fourths.

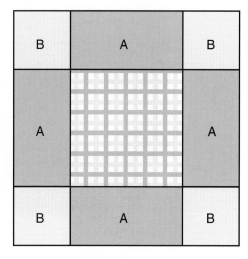

Figure 30. Background block assembly.

Scrappy Projects:
Black Cats and Folk Leaves Pillow

by Lorinda Lie

Materials

- Four 8" squares felted wool for pillow top
- Wool scraps for appliqué and tongues
- ½ yd. cotton for backing and lapped pillow back
- Embroidery floss
- Batting
- Freezer paper
- 14" pillow form

Patterns

Folk Leaf, page 81
Cat and Tongue, page 90
Penny Circle set A, page 93

Black Cats and Folk Leaves Pillow

Beginner/intermediate level
The tongue edging isn't difficult, but the finishing is more involved.
8" finished blocks, 14" pillow

This pillow would be pretty in a variety of colors for real or imaginary cats. The one pictured contains two wool fabrics for alternating background squares, plus scraps of two additional wool fabrics for the cats and leaves. It could easily be made from only two wool fabrics for an interesting positive-negative effect.

1 Prepare wool: If you are new to wool quilts, be sure to read Learning the Basics, pages 8–28, for directions on felting wool, and tips for how to work with it by hand or machine.

2 Cut appliqués: Trace the cat, folk leaf, and penny circle set A, on freezer paper. Cut the freezer-paper templates and iron them on wool. Cut two folk leaves, two cats, and one set of penny circles. To reverse the cat, turn one of the wool cats over.

3 Appliqué blocks: Place the leaves and cats toward the center of the pillow instead of centering them in each square (Basics, page 14). Appliqué the leaves and cats with the blanket stitch and three strands of floss. Save the penny circles for later.

4 Join blocks: Sew the finished blocks together with a ½" seam allowance. Press the seam allowances open. Blanket-stitch the penny circles in the center of the pillow.

5 Prepare tongues: Cut out and hand blanket-stitch the edges of 40 tongues, leaving the straight ends unstitched (page 26).

6 Finish pillow: Follow the directions on page 25 for a lapped back. Cut rectangles 11" x 15" and follow the directions for quilting and finishing a pillow with tongues, page 26. Quilt around each appliqué and ½" from seams.

Collecting Wool

For your first wool project, purchase anything you find that is within your price range. Look for a variety of colors. You will probably find camel, navy, and black fairly easily. Try to add a few plaids and brighter colors. Don't be overly concerned about whether all the colors go together. As in any scrap quilt, the greater the variety of colors, the more coordinated the piece will look.

Probably the best sources for small amounts of wool are quilt shops and quilt show merchant malls. Both often sell precut wool in varied colors and small amounts, such as ½ yard, ¼ yard, and even 12" squares. When small amounts are needed for projects such as pillows, this is an easy way to get the colors without overextending the checkbook.

Button Projects: **Button Quilt**

by Lorinda Lie

Button Quilt

Beginner level
42" x 72" topper or nap quilt
6" finished block

Try your hand at a small amount of blanket-stitch appliqué in this quick project. Because of the minimal appliqué and machine quilting, it makes a quick, personalized gift for a special person or occasion. The buttons "click" when you fold the quilt, making it a fun quilt to use.

Variations

• *Choose a different color palette to work with, perhaps the recipient's favorite color, or go wild and make a scrap quilt with a random palette.*

• *Tie the centers of the blocks that aren't appliquéd instead of using buttons to make this quilt suitable for a young child. Shorten the quilt to eight rows of seven blocks for a crib quilt, 42" x 48".*

Quilt Assembly

1 Prepare wool: If you are new to wool quilts, be sure to read Learning the Basics, pages 8–28, for directions on felting wool, and tips for how to work with it by hand or machine.

2 Cut squares: You will need 84 7" squares. Lay them out in 12 rows of seven squares each, balancing the colors, plaids, and solids evenly throughout the quilt.

3 Cut appliqués: Choose the name you want, and if it is longer than seven letters, run it vertically instead of horizontally. Follow the general pattern directions (page 14) to trace the letters and numbers on freezer paper and cut out the templates.

4 Appliqué blocks: Before sewing the blocks together, blanket-stitch the letters and numbers to the block by hand or machine.

5 Join blocks: Sew blocks together with a ½" seam allowance. Rather than sew long rows, sew four-block units, then sew four units together to make a larger unit, and so on. This method minimizes weight and makes the quilt easier to work with. Press all seam allowances open.

6 Quilt layers: Trim the selvages from the flannel and piece for the backing as shown in chart on page 28. Layer backing, batting, and top. Baste together with pins or thread. Machine quilt a generous ½" on each side of the seam allowances and around letters and numbers. Use a walking foot and loosen the pressure on your presser foot so the fabric layers feed evenly through the machine. Use an embroidery or darning foot to free-motion stitch around the letters and numbers.

7 Finish edges: Cut 3" strips of straight-grain cotton binding. Piece the strips together, end to end, on the diagonal. Fold in half, wrong sides together, and sew the strip to the right side of the quilt, taking a ½" seam allowance and mitering the corners. Hand-stitch binding to the back of the quilt and tack miters closed.

8 Add buttons: Sew a button, through all the layers, in the middle of each square that doesn't have an appliqué. Use the buttons you saved when you cut apart your garments after felting. For an extra-special somebody, this quilt provides a fun way to display old or antique buttons. Add a label and enjoy.

Materials (see Collecting Wool, page 28)

• 3½ yds. – variety of wool skirts or fabrics, in solids and plaids for a controlled palette
• 2⅔ yds. flannel for backing
• ⅞ yd. cotton for straight-grain binding
• Black embroidery floss
• 70-80 buttons, ¾" – 1" diameter
• Batting (Thermore, page 22)   • Freezer paper

Patterns

Alphabet and Numbers,
pages 101–110

——— Caution ———

Do not use buttons
for children under age 3.
They are a choking hazard.

Heart-Felt Wool Appliqué — Lorinda Lie

Button Projects:
Those Crazy Blues Vest

by Lorinda Lie

Materials

- Yardages will vary depending on pattern and size chosen
- Vest pattern of your choice, preferably with simple lines and no darts.
  (Vest pictured was adapted from a Carol Doak pattern, see bibliography (page 110)
- Variety of felted blue wool at least 7 or 8 different colors including stripes or plaids
- Muslin for foundation
- Cotton for lining
- 1 skein medium gray #5 perle cotton
- Heavy-duty spray starch
- Silver buttons for embellishment. (There are 23 buttons, front and back, on the vest pictured.)

Those Crazy Blues Vest

Beginner level

This is a loose-fitting, unquilted casual vest with a real folk look. It was embroidered by using the machine button-hole stitch throughout. The squares and rectangles are easy shapes to machine blanket stitch, making this an easy and quick project. A variety of threads was used, including rayon and metallic. All top threads were doubled, and the largest machine buttonhole stitch was used. The silver floral design was stitched with a machine-embroidery option before being sewn to the vest.

Variations
- *Use decorative machine stitches.*
- *Hand embroider crazy-pieced vest with either basic or fancy blanket stitches.*
- *Add more embroidered embellishments like silver design on vest front. Traditional crazy quilts are heavily embroidered.*

Vest Assembly

1 Prepare wool: If you are new to wool quilts, be sure to read Learning the Basics, pages 8–28, for directions on felting wool, and tips for how to work with it by hand or machine.

2 Prepare vest pattern: Straighten curved side seams if necessary. Remove the seam allowance on the neck, arm, front, and bottom edges. Lap front and back side seams to remove seam allowances so the vest can be made as one unit.

3 Prepare muslin base: With heavy spray starch, spray a large enough piece of muslin for two vest fronts and back. You may want to spray twice for a very stiff foundation. Press smooth when dry. No other stabilizer should be necessary. On the wrong side of the muslin, trace around the complete vest pattern to use as a placement guide for the wool piece.

Mark shoulder corners, center back, bottom, and arm hole edges on right side of the muslin, to use as a guide for pattern placement after the embroidery is finished.

4 Cut out a variety of sizes of squares and rectangles from blue wools and lay them on the muslin foundation. Keep pieces fairly large; use picture as a guide. Overlap pieces at least ½" and cover the pattern you drew on the muslin. Pin and machine baste wool pieces in place by using basting thread and a walking foot. Reduce pressure on the presser foot to keep pieces from stretching or shifting.

5 Embroider the crazy patches in place with the largest possible machine blanket stitch and double thread on top. Use a variety of threads and colors. High contrast colors such as light blues, medium and light gray, and silver will show best.

6 Pockets: If you want to make pockets for your vest, cut two pieces of wool 6½" x 8½". Cut two pieces of cotton lining fabric 6½" x 7½". Layer the pieces wrong sides together, matching sides and bottom. Fold 1" of wool to the back, covering the top edge of the lining. Machine blanket stitch on the right side of the pocket a scant 1" from the top.

7 Assembling the vest: Stitch the shoulder seams on the vest front. Pin pockets to vest fronts. Try on and adjust pocket placement if necessary. Pockets on THOSE CRAZY BLUES are purposely set off kilter.

8 Lining: Cut out vest lining the same way you traced the muslin foundation by removing the side seams and seam allowances on all openings. Sew shoulder seams on vest lining. (Note: for a more polished finish, instead of removing lining seam allowances, turn them under all around.)

Layer vest and lining wrong sides together matching all edges. Pin in place. Machine stitch ⅜" around all openings with navy thread for low contrast.

9 Finish vest by hand blanket stitching around all openings with #5 medium gray perle cotton and a large hand blanket stitch (bite ⅜", distance ¼"). This must be done by hand. The machine blanket stitch is not an edge stitch. Embellish with silver buttons.

Heart's Desire Projects:
Hearts 'n Wool Quilt

by Lorinda Lie

Hearts 'n Wool Quilt

Intermediate level – Precision cutting the plaids is easy, but it takes a little more time and more wool.

42" x 72" topper or nap quilt

6" finished blocks

HEARTS 'N WOOL is designed to be a day brightener any time of the year. It is a scrap quilt with a loose, monochromatic color scheme. The blocks are alternately plaid and solid. For that extra touch, the plaid background squares and plaid hearts are precision cut by using the lines of the plaids as design elements.

The primary color of this quilt is red, so the majority of your pieces need to "read" red. It will add richness and interest to include a variety of related colors, such as rose, purple, rust, and brown. You will probably find a greater variety of plaids at thrift stores than fabric stores. The greater the variety, the more interesting the quilt.

This is a great project to do with your children or grandchildren. Give them paper and crayons or scissors and ask them to draw or cut hearts for you in a variety of sizes and shapes. Asymmetrical hearts can be free-hand drawn or cut. Make symmetrical hearts by folding a piece of paper in half and cutting a half heart on the fold.

Variations

- *Use pink or purple for your predominant color, as in the PURPLE HEARTS! pillow, page 42.*
- *Use all solid colors, and fancy-stitch the hearts in contrasting colors. (See page 19 for stitches.)*
- *For a quicker project and more economical use of your wool stash, omit the precision cutting.*

Quilt Assembly

1 Prepare wool: If you are new to wool quilts, be sure to read Learning the Basics, pages 8–28, for directions on felting wool, and tips for how to work with it by hand or machine.

2 Cut squares: Look carefully at the picture of the quilt. Notice how the plaids in both the background squares and the hearts have been cut. You will need 84 7" background squares: 42 solid and 42 plaid.

3 Cut appliqués: You will need at least 84 hearts. At least half the hearts need to be plaids and the other half solid colors. Look at Figure 31 for ideas on how to precision cut from plaids. Precision cutting means taking special care in placing your templates on the fabric to take advantage of the design elements in the fabric. A variety of hearts has been included in the pattern section. If you would like other shapes or sizes, you can cut your own or use cookie cutters. When you have chosen 8 to 10 heart shapes, trace multiple freezer-paper templates by folding the paper and cutting through several layers at one time. Don't forget to include at least one heart and hand. Use the design in the pattern section (page 79) or draw around your helpers' hands or your own to include as special signature blocks.

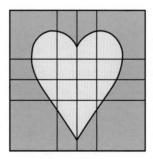 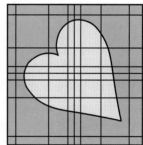

Figure 31. Place the templates on the plaids to take advantage of the fabric's design.

Materials

- Variety of wool skirts in red plaids and solids, or 2½ yds. plaid and 2½ yds. solid wool fabric. Quilt pictured has 23 different plaids and 13 solids.
- 2⅔ yds. flannel for backing
- ⅞ yd. cotton for straight-grain binding
- Assorted colors of embroidery floss to match or coordinate with wool fabric
- Batting (Thermore, page 22)   • Freezer paper

Patterns

Hearts, pages 78–80

Iron the hearts on the wool scraps, paying attention to the lines in the plaids to enhance the hearts. Use each heart template until it becomes too fuzzy to stick. Cut more templates as needed. Refer to the photograph of the quilt for ideas of ways to use multiple hearts in one block by stacking or overlapping them.

4 Appliqué blocks: Use the basic blanket stitch and three strands of coordinating embroidery floss to appliqué the hearts by hand or machine. Even if you are experienced in sewing blanket stitches, you may want to check the figures and instructions on page 16. If you prefer not to deal with sharp points and corners, you can round them slightly.

5 Join blocks: Arrange the blocks in an alternating plaid and solid pattern and disperse the fabrics throughout the quilt. Use a ½" seam allowance to sew the blocks together in two- and four-block units. Sew the units together, matching the intersections to finish the top. Use a walking foot and reduce the pressure slightly on your presser foot. Sew gently to avoid stretching the wool. Press all seam allowances open, using steam and a clapper, if you have one.

6 Layer quilt: Trim the selvages from the flannel and cut the backing into two 1⅓-yard pieces. Turn them and sew as shown in Figure 28 on page 28. Layer the backing, batting, and quilt top. Pin or thread baste the layers together.

7 Quilt layers: Quilt by machine or hand around the hearts and a scant ¾" on both sides of the seam lines. The quilt pictured was machine quilted with brown thread on the top and bottom. Brown is a good blender color with so many different reds.

8 Finish quilt: Cut 3" strips of cotton for straight-grain binding. Piece the strips together, end to end, on the diagonal. Fold the pieced strip in half lengthwise, wrong sides together, and sew the strip to the right side of the quilt with a ½" seam allowance. Miter the corners. Hand-stitch the binding to the back of the quilt and tack the miters closed. Label and enjoy.

Purple Hearts! Pillow

Intermediate level – fancy stitches
14" pillow

Wouldn't this be fun to make for a daughter or granddaughter? Age 9 or 10 seems to be about when the "purple passion" hits. The pillow is a nice, small project to showcase fancy embroidery stitches. Avoid plaids to let your stitches take the spotlight.

Variations

• *Make the pillow in reds or pinks for a Valentine's gift, or all in white and embroidered in silver and gold to commemorate a wedding or anniversary.*
• *Make the pillow in alternating solids and plaids as in the HEARTS 'N WOOL quilt. Use the basic blanket stitch to appliqué plaid hearts.*

Pillow Assembly

1 Prepare wool: If you are new to wool quilts, be sure to read Learning the Basics, pages 8–28, for directions on felting wool, and tips for how to work with it by hand or machine.

2 Cut appliqués: Trace heart shapes on freezer paper or draw your own. Cut out and press the templates on wool scraps and cut out the wool hearts. Place the wool appliqué hearts on the wool squares diagonally as shown in the photo.

3 Appliqué hearts: Appliqué the four large hearts with your choice of fancy stitches (page 19). Use a different stitch for each heart.

4 Add embroidery: Fill in the two remaining large hearts by sewing French knots in one and lazy-daisy flowers in the other for a calico look.

5 Join blocks: Sew the four blocks together with ½" seam allowances. Press seam allowances.

6 Finish pillow: Create a ruffle in coordinating calico fabric, following the directions on page 25. This pillow is not quilted. Using an 11" x 15" rectangle, make a lapped back (page 25).

Heart-Felt Wool Appliqué — Lorinda Lie

Heart's Desire Projects:
Purple Hearts! Pillow

by Sue Clemens

Materials

- Four 8" squares of felted wool in purples and fuchsias
- Scraps of felted wool in same colors for appliqué
- 1⅛ yds. coordinating calico cotton for pillow back and ruffle
- Embroidery floss in contrasting colors
- Freezer paper
- 14" pillow form

Patterns

Hearts, page 78

A Touch of Autumn Projects:
Falling Leaves Quilt

by Lorinda Lie, machine quilted by Peg Reis

Falling Leaves Quilt

Intermediate level – The sharp points take extra care but really aren't difficult.
42" x 72" topper or nap quilt
6" finished block

As the air gets crisper and the days shorter, enjoy an autumn walk in the leaves. Pick leaves from your favorite trees and bushes or use the templates provided to make this rich-looking quilt. Before you know it, you'll be curled up under it, enjoying its warmth on those long winter nights. FALLING LEAVES is made by using the rich complimentary colors of autumn in solid-colored wool fabrics with a stuffed binding for added comfort.

Variations
- *Use plaids as well as solids to give more texture.*
- *Round points for simpler appliquéing.*
- *Place a leaf in every other square for a smaller leaf pile to appliqué. Quilt a leaf shape in the blank blocks.*
- *Include a few squirrels preparing for winter or playing in the leaves.*

Quilt Assembly

1 Prepare wool: If you are new to wool quilts, be sure to read Learning the Basics, pages 8–28, for directions on felting wool, and tips for how to work with it by hand or machine.

2 Cut squares: Cut 84 7" squares and 84 leaves as follows: Cut the blocks first and use the scraps for leaves. Cut about half the blocks and leaves from green wools and a few browns and the other half from burgundy, plum, rust, and gold, plus a few browns. Using the brown wool helps tie all the colors together. It isn't

necessary to be that exact about how many blocks you cut from each color.

3 Cut appliqués: On freezer paper, trace the leaves you have collected or use the leaves in the pattern section. Cut several freezer-paper templates of each leaf. Iron the paper on the wool and cut the leaves. See Figure 34, page 49, if you are cutting plaid leaves.

4 Arrange appliqués: When you have most of your leaves and blocks cut, arrange the blocks and scatter the leaves so the colors and leaf shapes are balanced. Finish cutting the last few blocks and leaves according to the colors you need for balance. Try not to have too many of the same leaf shape next to each other. Rotate the leaves randomly on the blocks to provide a sense of motion. If you have a large enough work area or design wall, lay out the entire quilt and then walk away from it. Take several days to adjust and readjust colors until you are happy with the final arrangement.

5 Identify blocks: As you pin or staple leaves in place, number each block so you know where it fits in the quilt and how the leaf is oriented (Figure 32, page 46). Number the rows consistently, so that when you are standing at the bottom of the quilt, all the numbers face you regardless of what direction the leaf is turned. Take a photograph of your layout to help you remember.

6 Appliqué leaves: Appliqué the leaves, using the basic blanket stitch, page 16. Embroider a few leaves with variegated floss or perle cotton for added interest (Photo 2). Scatter these special leaves evenly over the quilt.

Materials (See Collecting Wool, page 28)
- Variety of wool garments in autumn colors, or 3½ yds. wool fabric for background blocks and 1½ yds. for leaves. Quilt contains approximately 20 different colors or garments.
- 2⅔ yds. flannel for backing
- ⅔ yd. cotton for stuffed binding
- Assorted colors of embroidery floss to match leaves
- One skein variegated floss or perle cotton in autumn colors
- Batting (Quilt was made with pre-washed wool batting.)
- Freezer paper

Patterns
Leaves, pages 47, 81–83
Squirrels, page 84

---

7 Join blocks: Lay out the quilt. Make any final adjustments in block placement and orientation. Sew the blocks together by using a walking foot and ½" seam allowance. Steam press seam allowances open.

8 Layer quilt: Trim selvages from the backing fabric and cut into two 1⅓-yard pieces. Turn and sew them as shown in Figure 18, page 23. If you are using wool batting, gently prewash it in warm water and dry it in your dryer just until dry to preshrink it. Layer the backing, batting, and top; baste.

9 Quilt layers: The quilt pictured was commercially quilted in free-motion gentle waves to reinforce the idea of falling leaves (Figure 33). Where additional quilting is needed to fulfill the batting requirements, outline an occasional leaf and tack the block intersections. Quilting with variegated thread will add sparkle and motion to the quilt. This quilt is best machine quilted.

10 Finish edges: A stuffed binding makes a nice frame for this quilt (page 24).

11 Label quilt: Don't forget to label your quilt with your name, date, town, state, year, and any other information you would like to include, such as the type of batting or washing instructions.

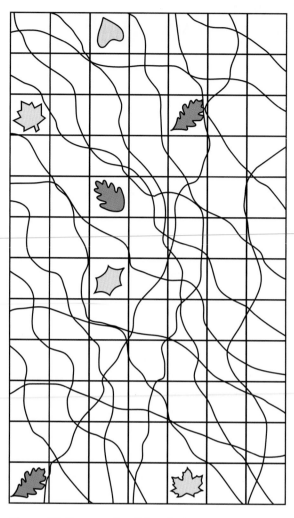

Figure 33. Suggested quilting design.

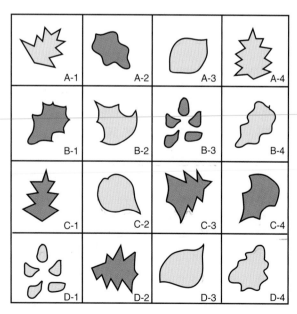

Figure 32. Number the blocks by rows with leaves in desired position.

Photo 2. Leaf embroidered with variegated perle cotton embroidery floss.

Heart-Felt Wool Appliqué — Lorinda Lie

Leaf Patterns

More leaf patterns can be found on pages 81–83.

Red Bud

Silver Maple

Red Oak

Heart-Felt Wool Appliqué — *Lorinda Lie*

A Touch of Autumn Projects:
Wreath of Leaves Pillow

by Jean Glise

Materials

- 15" square of solid-colored felted wool
- Scraps of felted plaid wool
- Embroidery floss to coordinate with colors in the plaid wool
- ½ yd. cotton for backing and lapped pillow back
- ¼ yd. cotton for 3" straight-grain binding
- Batting • Freezer paper • 14" pillow form
- Three leather buttons with shanks

Patterns

Red Oak Leaf, page 47
Leaf quilting pattern, page 81

Wreath of Leaves Pillow

Intermediate level – Precision cutting and sharp points
14" pillow

There are several different realistic leaves in the pattern section, any of which would make a charming pillow.

Variations

- *Use a different leaf for your wreath.*
- *Use a plaid background and leaves of solid colors.*
- *Gently round the leaf points for easier appliqué.*

Quilt Assembly

1 Prepare wool: If you are new to wool quilts, be sure to read Learning the Basics, pages 8–28 for directions on felting wool, and tips for how to work with it by hand or machine.

2 Cut appliqués: Cut eight red-oak leaves from the plaid wool. Use the lines of the plaid to suggest veins in the leaves (Figure 34).

3 Appliqué leaves: Arrange the leaves in a tight circle to form a wreath on 15" wool square. The inside diameter of the circle should be approximately 2". Blanket stitch the leaves in place by hand or machine.

4 Quilt pillow: Layer pillow top, batting, and backing. Machine or hand quilt around the leaves in the wreath. Hand quilt a small leaf in each corner. For a bolder look, double the quilting thread or use size 8 or 12 perle cotton.

5 Finish pillow: Follow the directions, page 25, to make the pillow back. Cut rectangles 11" by 15".

6 Bind edges: Cut 3" strips for straight-grain binding. Fold the strips in half lengthwise and bind the pillow as you would a quilt. Sew button "acorns" in place in the center of the wreath.

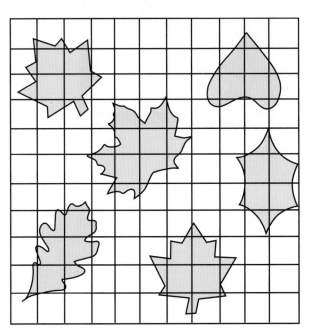

Figure 34. When cutting the leaves, use the plaids to indicate leaf veins.

Fall Jacket by Lorinda Lie (back view). Appliquéd leaves were added to a purchased wool jacket. Garments are a bit awkward to hold, and it takes some care to avoid stitching through the lining, but the results are worth the extra effort.

Hawaiian Style Cutwork Projects:
Primary Bulbs Wallhanging

by Lorinda Lie

Materials (See Collecting Wool, page 28)

- One lavender or purple skirt or ⅝ yd. fabric for hyacinth
- Two or three yellow skirts or 1⅛ yds. of fabric for daffodils
  (Yellow can be hard to find and may need to be purchased.)
- Two or three red skirts or 1⅛ yds. for tulips
- Five or six black skirts or 2 yds. of black wool   • Freezer paper
- 3 yds. cotton for backing   • ⅝ yd. cotton for straight-grain binding
- Yellow, red and purple embroidery floss to match wool for appliqué
- One ball #12 black perle cotton for quilting   • Batting (Thermore, page 22)

Patterns

Tulip, page 96
Tulip Center, page 96
Hyacinth, page 97
Daffodil, page 98
Quilting design, page 80

Primary Bulbs Wallhanging

Intermediate level – The larger blocks and more intricate shapes are a little more difficult but are still much easier than needle-turn appliqué.

48" x 48" wallhanging

16" finished block

This striking wallhanging is sure to be a crowd pleaser. Wool is an ideal medium for any quilter who loves the look of Hawaiian cutwork but is reluctant to try the fine needle-turn appliqué required to make a traditional Hawaiian quilt. No edges need to be turned to make this beautiful wallhanging. Just cut and sew. Let the vibrant colors of wool reflect the bright colors of Hawaiian quilts as this traditional style goes folk-art for easier appliqué. The print binding, large quilting stitch, coarse thread, as well as the quilted hearts, all enhance the folk-art look.

Variations
- *Make each design in two colors, green for the foliage and primary colors for the flowers.*
- *For a softer look, make the flowers in pastel colors on a white background.*

Quilt Assembly

1 Prepare wool: If you are new to wool quilts, be sure to read Learning the Basics, pages 8–28, for directions on felting wool, and tips for how to work with it by hand or machine.

2 Cut squares: Cut nine 17" background squares from black felted wool. Cut 15" squares for flowers as follows: four red, four yellow, one lavender.

3 Make templates: Cut five 15" squares of freezer paper. Fold the paper into eighths as you would to cut a snowflake (Figure 35). Trace one hyacinth, two tulip, and two daffodil patterns on the top triangles of the folded freezer-paper squares. Staple each wedge together and cut out the designs. Be careful not to skew the design as you cut.

4 Cut appliqués: Open the paper designs carefully and press them on the 15" colored squares. Reuse the freezer paper as necessary to cut four red tulips, four yellow daffodils, and one purple hyacinth.

Do not attempt to fold and cut the wool as you did the freezer paper. The wool is too heavy, and it will not cut accurately when folded. Small sharp embroidery scissors or manicure scissors are helpful for cutting the intricate designs.

5 Baste appliqués: With a chalk marker, draw diagonal and median lines on background squares to mirror folds of freezer paper. Working a square at a time, with freezer paper still in place, center the wool flowers matching the folds of the freezer paper with the chalk guide lines on the background square. Carefully remove the freezer paper, pinning as you go. Adjust the appliqué if necessary. Baste the flowers in place.

Don't skip basting. The laciness of the design coupled

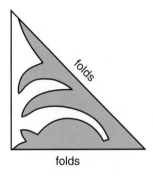

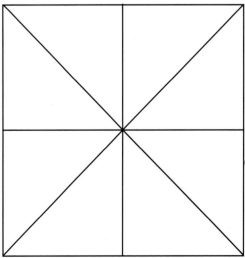

Figure 35. Fold paper into eighths; trace and cut pattern.

with the stretchiness of the wool make it too easy for the appliqué piece to shift if it is only pinned in place. Nice Hawaiian work is very symmetrical in its design and placement.

6 Appliqué blocks: Use the basic blanket stitch to appliqué the blocks. Sharp points (page 17) will give this wallhanging a crisper, more traditional look.

Appliqué the inside of the daffodils first, then the outside. Appliqué the penny circles in the center of the tulip and daffodil blocks last.

7 Join blocks: Arrange the blocks with the hyacinth in the center. Sew the blocks together with a ½" seam allowance. Press seam allowances open.

8 Quilt layers: Piece quilt back. Layer with batting and backing, and baste. Use #12 perle cotton and take larger stitches (6–8 per inch). You will need to use a #7 or #8 Between needle to accommodate the larger thread. Quilt around each appliqué next to the stitching and again about ½" outside it, Hawaiian-style.

This technique is sometimes called "echo quilting." Quilt inside each cutout and around the penny circles. Quilt the hyacinth as indicated on the pattern.

Quilt a double heart design in the spaces between the tulip leaves. Center the hearts in the spaces, crossing over the seam allowances next to the hyacinth and daffodils. On the outside edge, quilt partial hearts in the spaces between the tulip leaves letting the quilting design run off the edge.

9 Finish quilt: Cut 3" strips of cotton for straight-grain binding and piece the strips together, end to end, on the diagonal. Fold the pieced strip in half lengthwise, wrong sides together, and sew the strip to the right side of the quilt with a ½" seam allowance. Miter the corners. Hand-stitch the binding to the back of the quilt and tack the miters closed. Add a label to your wallhanging and enjoy.

Warm Welcome Wallhanging

Intermediate level
The larger blocks and more intricate shapes are more challenging.
16" x 48" wallhanging
16" finished blocks

WARM WELCOME is a wonderful oxymoron – a Hawaiian-style wallhanging made of fabric more suited to Alaska! The name comes from the warm wool fabric and the pineapple design symbolizing hospitality in Hawaii.

Variations
• *Make a Hawaiian quilt by alternating these two patterns or add additional Hawaiian designs.*
• *Make a snowflake wallhanging or quilt with these same techniques. Enlist your children or grandchildren to help you cut snowflakes to make this a family project. Keep your snowflakes fairly large and simple to adapt them to wool.*

Quilt Assembly
Use the plumeria and pineapple designs for this quilt. Follow paper folding and cutting instructions for the PRIMARY BULBS wallhanging. Make one plumeria of color A and two pineapples of color B.

The pineapple design has cutouts on the leaves and in the center. The plumeria design has penny circles added on top. Cut these extra circles from scraps of leftover wool.

Hawaiian Style Cutwork Projects:
Warm Welcome Wallhanging

by Lorinda Lie

Materials (See Collecting Wool, page 28)

- Three skirts of color A or ⅔ yd. wool fabric
- Three skirts of color B or ⅔ yd. wool fabric
- 1 yd. cotton fabric for backing
- ⅜ yd. cotton fabric in color A for straight-grain binding
- Embroidery floss to match wool fabrics
- Batting (Thermore, page 22)
- Freezer paper

Patterns

Plumeria, page 99
Pineapple Center, page 100
Pineapple, page 100

"Bestest" Projects from Worsted Wool:
Fan Dance Quilt

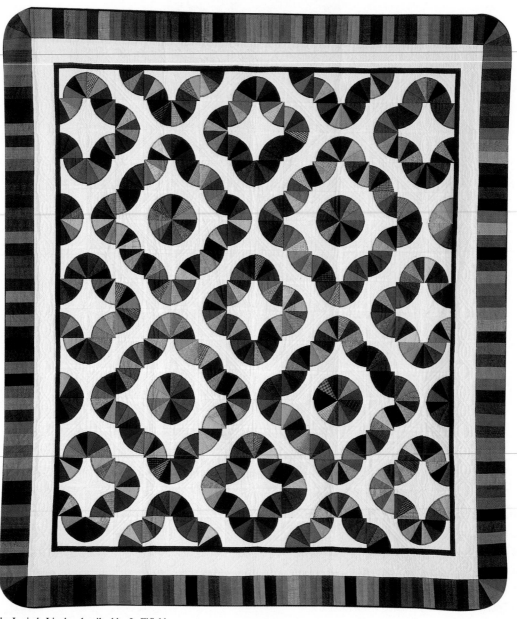

by Lorinda Lie, hand quilted by Jo Fifield

Fan Dance Quilt

Beginner level
90" x 100" queen-sized quilt
5" finished block

This elegant quilt is made completely of men's suits. It is foundation paper pieced and appliquéd to muslin squares. The small size of the squares makes it an easy carry-around project. Purchase old suits at thrift shops or raid the closet of the man in your life for suits that are getting worn.

If you need to purchase garments for this project, look for worsted-weight wool and men's trousers as it is generally lighter weight and will piece with less bulk. Fabric that is 80% wool or less can be used for this project.

While you are at the resale shop, pick up an old plate that measures 9¼" in diameter to use with your rotary cutter to trim the curved edges of the fans.

Variations

- *Embroider the quilt with red perle cotton and sew red buttons at the center of the fans to add color.*
- *Design your own setting for the fans.*

Quilt Assembly

1 Prepare wool: If you are new to wool quilts, be sure to read Learning the Basics, pages 8–28, for directions on felting wool, and tips for how to work with it by hand or machine. While worsted wool and wool blends do not felt or shrink as nicely as 100% wool, it is still important to put them through the felting process so that your quilt will be washable when it's finished.

NOTE: Follow the directions for the projects in this section carefully. Some of the seam allowances and pressing instructions vary from other projects.

2 Cut fans and border rectangles: It may be helpful to use a pinking blade in your rotary cutter because blends and worsted wools ravel easily. If using pants, cut one pant leg crosswise into 6" strips for the border. Cut the other leg crosswise into 5" strips for the fans.

A large pair of pants will yield approximately 41 large rectangles and 47 small rectangles per leg. A small pair of pants will yield approximately 28 large rectangles and 35 small ones per leg. It is okay to include a seam in the larger rectangles for the pieced outside border. To eliminate bulk, the smaller rectangles should not have seams.

For the center fan blocks, cut 672 rectangles 3" wide from the 5" strips. For the corner fans, cut 12 rectangles 3½" wide from the 6" strips. For the border, cut 170 rectangles 3" wide from the 6" strips.

3 Cut muslin: Remove selvages and square the ends of the muslin. With a rotary cutter, cut an 82½" piece of yardage from the 8 yards of muslin (Figure 36, page 56). Cut two strips along the length of this piece 4¾" wide. Label each one "side border" and set aside. Cut two strips 4¾" by 81". Label these "top and bottom border" and set aside. Cut the remainder of this piece of muslin into 39 6" squares. From the other piece of yardage, cut 31 6" rows. Cut each row into six 6" squares, which will yield 186 squares for a total of 225 squares. There will be one extra.

4 Cut black border and binding: Cut eight strips of black fabric across the grain, 1¾" wide by approximately 40" long. Set aside for the borders. Use the remainder to cut 3"-wide bias binding strips. Sew the strips together, end to end, with a diagonal seam. You will need a continuous strip approximately 360" for the double-fold bias binding.

Materials (See Collecting Wool, page 28)

- 8 yds. 45"-wide muslin
- Suit swatches and pant-leg scraps from hems; 12–15 pairs of men's trousers; 8 yds. worsted wool, wool blends, or wool suiting in gray, brown, black, and olive in solids, stripes, and plaids
- 1⅜ yds. black fabric for sashing and binding
- Eight skeins (27 yds. each) black #5 DMC perle cotton
- Batting. (Quilt shown has wool batting.)   • Tracing paper for foundation piecing

Patterns

Fans, page 94

5 Foundation piece fans: Use the rectangles of wool randomly. Do not match for color or weight. The overall effect is a rich, scrappy look.

Copy, trace, or print 224 paper foundations for the center fans and four paper foundations for the corner fans. Follow the steps to paper piece the fans.

6 Appliqué blocks: Tear away paper and place each fan on a 6" muslin square, aligning the straight edges of the fan with the corner of the square. Use a large stitch to machine baste the curved edge of the fan to the muslin.

With black perle cotton, blanket-stitch the curved edge of the fan to the muslin (Figure 37). Make the bite and distance about ⅜". Or machine blanket stitch the curved edge with doubled thread and a fairly large stitch. Remove the basting stitches.

7 Join blocks: Lay out the quilt on the floor or a design wall. Sew blocks with a ½" seam allowance into two block units, sewing from dot to dot as shown in Figure 17. Press seam allowances in alternating directions by row.

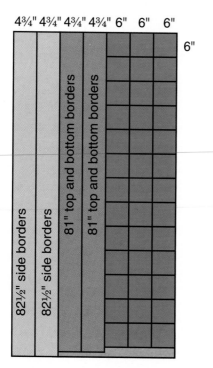

Figure 36. Muslin cutting guide.

Paper-Piecing Fans

Step 1
Place wool rectangle A under section A of the foundation, with the wrong side of the rectangle against the unmarked side of the paper.

Step 2
Fold back the foundation along the line between A and B, and with a rotary cutter or scissors, trim the rectangle, leaving a ¼" seam allowance. Unfold the foundation.

Step 3
Align rectangle B with the cut edge of A, right sides together. Holding the pieces in place, sew along the line between sections A and B. Use a small stitch and back-tack at both ends of the line. Do not sew beyond the end of the line.

Step 4
Press piece B open. Fold the foundation back along the line between B and C. Trim rectangle B, leaving a ¼" seam allowance. Unfold the foundation.

Step 5
Align rectangle C with the cut edge of B, right sides together. Sew the second seam as before.

Step 6
Press C open. Trim the last edge and curve of the fan, following the foundation as a guide. You can use an old plate with a 9¼" diameter to rotary cut the curve or trim with scissors. Trim excess bulk from seams in point of fan.

Heart-Felt Wool Appliqué — Lorinda Lie

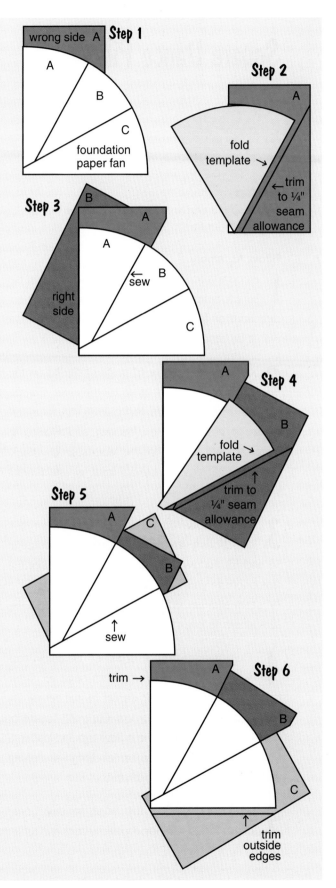

Step 1

wrong side   A

A

B

C

foundation
paper fan

Step 2

A

fold
template →

← trim
to ¼"
seam
allowance

Step 3

B

A

A

B
← sew

right
side

C

Step 4

A

B

fold →
template

↑
trim to
¼" seam
allowance

Step 5

A

C

B

↑
sew

Step 6

trim →   A

B

C

↑
trim
outside
edges

Join rows in four-block units, sewing dot to dot through the center intersection. Press seams, spinning seam allowances to reduce bulk at the intersection (Figure 38). Sew four-block units together, continuing in the same manner until the quilt top is pieced.

8 Sew borders: Piece 1¾" black border strips together, end to end, with diagonal seams to make two strips 81" long for the sides and two strips 72½" long for the top and bottom. Sew a strip on each side of the quilt top and then on the top and bottom with a ½" seam allowance. Press seam allowances toward the black.

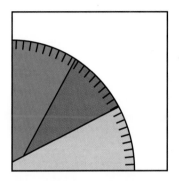

Figure 37. Blanket-stitch the curved edge of fan.

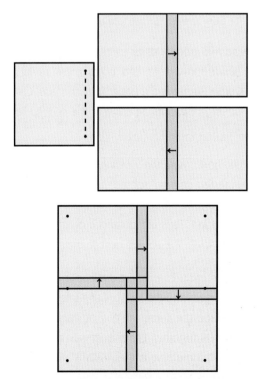

Figure 38. Press seam allowances in alternate directions by row. Join rows in four block units, sewing dot to dot. Press seams, "spinning" seam allowances in one direction.

Sew the 82½" long muslin border to the sides of the quilt with a ¼" seam allowance. (Note: Change in seam allowance width.) Press allowances toward the black. Sew the 81" muslin borders to the top and bottom in the same way. Press toward the black.

To make the pieced outer borders, sew the 3" x 6" wool rectangles together with a ½" seam allowance. Make two of the strips 81" long and two 91" long. Sew the 91" border strips to the long sides of the quilt with a ½" seam allowance. Pink the edges of the seam allowance to reduce fraying. Press toward the muslin border.

Paper piece four corner fans, following the directions for the center fans. Stay-stitch the curved edges. Leave the paper in place and sew one fan on each end of the 81" top and bottom border strips (Figure 39).

Top border

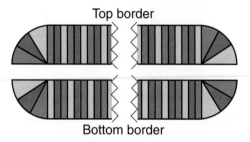

Bottom border

Figure 39. Sew fans to the top and bottom border strips.

Sew these two border strips to the quilt. Pink the edges of the seam allowances and press them toward the muslin border. Remove the paper from the fans. Carefully zigzag or serge the outside edge of the quilt to reduce fraying and to stabilize the corners.

9 Mark quilt: Mark the quilting pattern on the top. Suggested patterns for the muslin border and centers are on page 95. The lines down the muslin rows are quilted ½" apart. Fans are quilted around the curve of the fan and down the spokes next to the seam.

10 Finish quilt: To prepare the backing, remove the selvages from the fabric. Cut it into three lengths 96" long. Piece the three lengths of backing together. Baste the layers together. Hand quilt with a natural color of thread. Bind the raw edges with 3"-wide, double-fold bias binding (page 23). Label quilt.

Square Dance Pillow

Beginner level
20" pillow

Add a Fan pillow or two to create an ensemble for your bedroom. Pillows make nice presents, too.

Variation
• *Expand the design to make pillow shams to match the FAN DANCE quilt.*

Pillow Assembly

1 Prepare wool: If you are new to wool quilts, be sure to read Learning the Basics, pages 8–28, for directions on felting wool, and tips for how to work with it by hand or machine.

2 Cut pieces: Cut five 5" strips of muslin on the cross grain and set aside for the ruffle. Cut sixteen 6" muslin squares for pillow top, one 23" square of muslin for pillow backing, and two muslin rectangles 21" by 16" for the lapped pillow back. Cut 48 rectangles, 3" by 5", from worsted wool scraps for fans.

3 Make pillow: To make the fans, follow the directions given for the FAN DANCE quilt on page 56 and 57. Follow the picture for the layout of the fans or create your own. Sew blocks together with a ½" seam allowance from dot to dot and press the allowances to one side. (Figure 38, page 57).

4 Quilt layers: Mark the center of the pillow top with the quilting design from page 95. Draw lines ½" apart down the center of the remaining muslin rows across the corners. Cut a 22" square of batting and layer it with the pillow top and backing. Machine or hand quilt the center design and along the spokes and curve of each fan.

5 Finish pillow: See the finishing directions, pages 25–26, for lapped pillow back and ruffle.

"Bestest" Projects from Worsted Wool:
Square Dance Pillow

by Kathy Napientek and Deb Jaeger

Materials

- 2½ yds. muslin for square, ruffle, backing, and lapped back
- Scraps of men's suits or worsted wool scraps, felted
- Two skeins #5 black perle cotton
- Batting
- Tracing paper for foundation piecing

Patterns

Fans, page 94

Spring Fever Projects:
Tulip Garden Wallhanging

by Lorinda Lie

Tulip Garden Wallhanging

Intermediate level – Both the piecing and the appliqué are a bit complex but still not difficult.

36" x 48" wallhanging

January is when I get my first spell of spring fever. By then I'm tired of the dark colors of late fall and early winter, and the Christmas season is over. My heart yearns for sunshine and flowers, bird song, and warm bright colors. Each of these projects says "spring" in its own way. Tulips bloom in the elegant Tulip Garden wallhanging and the perky Springtime vest. Posies abound on the Two Cats in a Posy Patch pillow. Spend a cold January evening curled up cozily with your warm wool fabric, stitching up one of these floral bouquets.

The vibrant, intense colors of this wallhanging give it a stained-glass look. Bring spring into your home all year around with this elegant quilt. Use muted colors for a more classic, softer look.

Because of the shapes and sizes needed for the center square and outer border, purchase this yardage new. It may be as easy or economical to purchase small squares of assorted colors for the tulips at a quilt shop.

Variations

- *Use more neutral colors, such as beige and gray. Make the tulips cream colored for a more classic look.*
- *Use a textured fabric or small plaid in the triangles for a sportier country look.*
- *Instead of tulips, make a holly wreath, wreath of leaves, or some other design in the center square.*

- *Repeat your theme in the triangles, or leave them plain and use a quilted motif there instead of appliqué.*
- *Quilt a grid behind the tulips instead of echo quilting.*

Quilt Assembly

1 Prepare wool: If you are new to wool quilts, be sure to read Learning the Basics, pages 8–28, for directions on felting wool, and tips for how to work with it by hand or machine. Remember to remove the selvages before felting new wool.

2 Make triangle template: To make a template for the corner triangles, start with a 14" square of freezer paper. Draw a ½" seam allowance on the bottom and one side. On the inside line, measure 11½" on each allowance for two legs of a right triangle. Draw the third side of the triangle. Add ½" seam allowance to the third side (Figure 40). Draw three more triangles the same way. These triangles finish 11½" on the short sides.

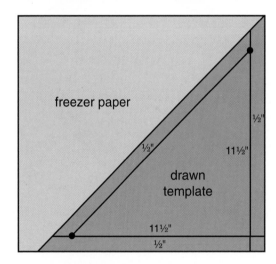

Figure 40. Make a freezer-paper template for the corner triangles.

Materials (See Collecting Wool, page 28)

- 1¾ yds. dark navy wool for center square and outer border
- One skirt or equivalent of ⅓ yd. forest green wool
- One skirt or equivalent of ½ yd. pale pink wool
- Scraps of green, purples, gold, and fuchsia wool for tulips
- Scraps of green for leaves and stems
- 1½ yds. cotton backing
- 1"–2" and 5" commercial cable quilting patterns
- ½ yd. purple cotton for 3" straight-grain binding
- Freezer paper
- Embroidery floss to match colors in tulips and leaves
- Batting (Thermore, page 22)

Patterns

Tulips and Leaves, pages 89–92

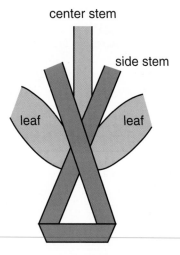

center stem

side stem

leaf   leaf

Figure 41. Trim border even with triangle.

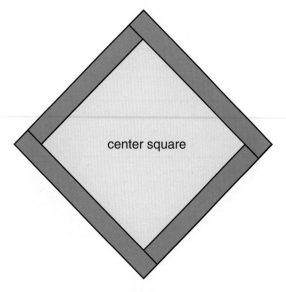

center square

Figure 42. Sew the green border to the center square.

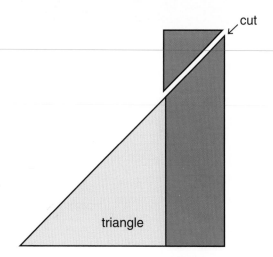

cut

triangle

Figure 43. Trim border even with triangle.

3 Cut pieces: From navy wool, cut a 20" square and two pieces, 7" x 36", for the outer border top and bottom. Cut four pieces 7" x 19½ " for the outer side borders.

Cut two pieces of forest green wool 3⅞" x 20" and two pieces 3⅞" x 26" for inner border. Note: While photo of wallhanging shows a mitered border, directions are given for a "butted" border, for ease of construction and reduction of bulk. Cut four pink triangles by using freezer paper templates pressed on pink wool.

4 Cut appliqués: Trace the patterns for the tulips and leaves. Remember, to reverse the designs, just turn the cut appliqué piece over unless the wool has a definite right and wrong side. Each of the three center tulips requires four pieces: A, A reversed, B, and C. Cut three of each piece. You will also need two F leaves and two G leaves. One of each will be reversed.

Each of the four tulips in the triangles requires five pieces: flower pieces D, D reversed, and E; leaves H and I. Cut sets of the five pieces for two of the corners. Reverse all the pieces and cut sets for the other two corners, which are mirror images.

Cut ½"-wide pieces of leaf green on the straight grain for stems as follows: Cut center stem 16" long. Cut a piece 22½" long for the two lower tulips. Cut four stems 7½" long for the tulips in the triangles.

5 Appliqué stems, leaves, and flowers: Arrange the appliqué pieces on the center square and corner triangles by using the photograph as a placement guide. Be careful on the corner triangles not to place pieces too close to the seam. Baste the pieces in place. The size and shape of these pieces make them easy to skew during stitching if basting is skipped. The pieces are also easier to hold and embroider without pins in the way.

Appliqué the pieces before sewing the wallhanging together. Blanket stitch all the pieces with matching thread, using the basic blanket stitch and a bite and distance of ⅛". Sharp points will give the tulips a crisp look (page 17).

Heart-Felt Wool Appliqué — Lorinda Lie

To appliqué center tulips, stitch leaves, then stems, and last, flowers. The slightly curved stems for side tulips are made from one piece folded at the bottom into a loop (Figure 41). The stem from the side tulips covers the bottom of the central stem. To appliqué the triangle tulips, curve the stems slightly. Stitch stems, leaves, then tulips. Note the direction that the tulip petals are lapped.

6 Join pieces: Use a walking foot and reduce the pressure on the presser foot. All seam allowances are a scant ½". Press all allowances open except the top and bottom ones on the outer border. Sew green border strips to the center square with butted corners (Figure 42).

Sew a short border strip to each pink triangle. Note that two triangles are mirror images. Trim the borders even with the long sides of the triangles as shown in Figure 43.

Sew two triangle units to adjacent sides of the center square (Figure 44). Handle wool very gently to avoid stretching the bias edges; pin well. Support the weight of the wool as you sew. Press seam allowances open.

Sew a border strip to the bottom (Figure 45). Press the allowances away from the center square.

Repeat the last two steps with the remaining triangle units and top border.

7 Quilt wallhanging: Layer the backing, batting, and top together and baste the layers. Quilt around the center tulips and echo quilt to fill the rest of the center square. Quilting with a dark green thread will make your stitches easier to see as you work. Mark the green border with chalk, soapstone pencil, or pouncing tool, using 1"–2" commercial cable pattern. Spray with hair spray to retain a chalk pattern. Re-mark as necessary.

Quilt the pink triangles the same way you did the center square. Quilt the navy border with a 5" commercial cable pattern and dark green thread.

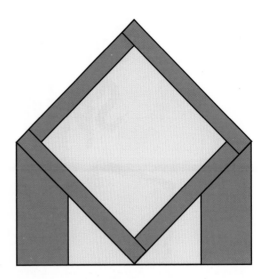

Figure 44. Sew triangle units in place.

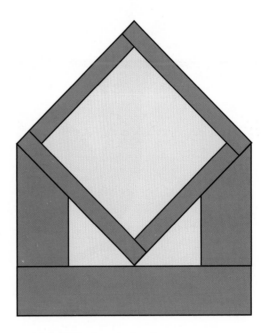

Figure 45. Add the bottom border.

8 Finish edges: Cut binding strips 3" wide on the straight grain. Sew the strips together, end to end, with a diagonal seam. Fold the resulting strip in half, wrong sides together, and sew the strip on the front of the quilt with a ½" seam allowance. Fold the binding over the raw edge and hand stitch in place on the back. Add a label to the wallhanging.

Spring Fever Projects:
Springtime Vest

by Lorinda Lie. This vest was adapted from
Easy Reversible Vests by Carol Doak.

Materials (See Collecting Wool, page 28)
- Yardages given are for vest pictured. Amounts may vary depending on pattern and size chosen.
- Vest pattern of your choice, preferably one without darts
- Two to three skirts, equivalent to 1 yd. 60" wool fabric in spring colors
- 1½ yds. cotton for vest backing
- ¾ yd. cotton for bias binding (2½")
- Assorted wool scraps
- Freezer paper
- Assorted embroidery floss in colors to match wool

Patterns
Sun, page 77
Heart Posy Leaf, page 78

Springtime Vest

Beginner level

This vest is constructed of recycled wool with wool appliqués and cotton backing. Leave out the batting for a vest that will take the chill off the cool evenings of early spring without being too warm for daytime wear. Use your favorite vest pattern and follow the ideas suggested here for decoration. (Vest shown was adapted from a Carol Doak pattern, see bibliography.)

Variations

- *Make vest fronts and back all one color instead of three.*
- *Make a vest for each season or holiday. Cookie cutters make handy templates for seasonal designs.*
- *Line vest with Thermore™ batting for added warmth.*
- *Omit binding and backing. Blanket-stitch all the edges for a real folk look.*
- *Sew vest fronts and back together and turn the vest instead of binding the edges. Machine stitch around the opening ½" from edge.*

Vest Assembly

1 Prepare wool: If you are new to wool quilts, be sure to read Learning the Basics, pages 8–28, for directions on felting wool, and tips for how to work with it by hand or machine. If you are using new wool, don't forget to remove the selvages before felting.

2 Cutting vest: How you cut this vest depends on the wool you have. The vest pictured was made from two skirts and one purchased piece of yellow wool yardage. The green skirt was very small, so the front and back of the skirt were pieced together on the straight grain to make a big enough piece of wool to cut the back. The back was deliberately cut off center so the seam became a design feature instead of just the center back seam.

Cut vest fronts and back from wool. To alter a pattern to use bias binding like the vest shown, trim seam allowances from neck, front, armholes, and bottom. Slightly round the sharp points on the front of the vest and center-back bottom edge. This vest was bound rather than turned for a smoother edge. The multi-colored cotton binding helps unify the three colors of the vest.

Cut the vest lining from cotton by using the same pattern pieces. Cut 2½" (⅜" finished) bias binding from cotton fabric. Amount will depend on pattern used.

3 Cut appliqués: Cut 6 posies and posy centers, 8 hearts for posy leaves (cutting from 2 colors will add interest), 1 sun (2 pieces), tulips and leaves from TULIP GARDEN WALLHANGING as follows: 2 each of Tulip pieces A, A reversed, and B; 2 F, 1G, 1H; and a strip of wool 16" long and ⅜" wide for stems.

4 Appliqué vest: Arrange appliqués on vest front and back panel, following the pictures as guides. Both F Leaves go on vest back. G and H go on front. Adjust pieces as necessary to fit your chosen vest. Pin or staple pieces in place. Pin pieces together at the shoulders and sides. Try on the vest to check the placement of the appliqué pieces. Arrange pieces in a way that flatters your body shape and size without any uncomfortable "bull's eyes." Appliqué the pieces with the basic blanket stitch and three strands of matching floss.

5 Assemble vest: Sew wool vest fronts to back at shoulders and sides. Press seam allowances open. Do the same with the vest lining. Pin the vest and lining wrong sides together.

6 Finish edges: Cut binding strips 2½" wide on the bias. Sew strips together, end to end, with a diagonal seam. Fold resulting strip in half, wrong sides together. Sew binding on the right side of the vest around all the openings, mitering corners as necessary. Hand tack in place on the inside.

7 Add quilting and embroidery. Quilt down the center of the tulip leaves to add dimension to the vest. Embroider the tulip centers with French knots and long, straight stitches. Embroider stems of posies with back stitch, page 19.

Spring Fever Projects:
Two Cats in a
Posy Patch Pillow

by Lorinda Lie

Materials

- 15" square felted navy wool
- Scraps of felted pastel wool
- ½ yd. cotton for stuffed binding
- Navy embroidery floss
- 15" square batting and scraps for binding
- Freezer paper

Patterns

Cat, page 90
Posy and Leaf, page 91

Two Cats in a Posy Patch Pillow

Beginner level
14" square finished

Pillow Assembly

1 Prepare wool: If you are new to wool quilts, be sure to read Learning the Basics, pages 8-28, for directions on felting wool, and tips for how to work with it by hand or machine.

2 Cut appliqués: Cut one cat and several posies, posy centers, and small posy leaves from freezer paper. You can reuse these templates until they get fuzzy.

Iron freezer paper on scraps of felted pastel wool and cut out appliqués. Remember that you do not need to reverse the cat pattern on freezer paper. Simply turn one cat over to reverse it after it is cut out of wool. Cut two wool cats, one dark gray and one white. Cut a total of 12 posies in several colors, 9 posy centers, and 13 leaves.

3 Appliqué pieces: Arrange the design following general placement in the photograph. Part of the white cat's tail hides under the posies. A posy covers the gray cat's foot. Its tail loops around on top of the same posy. Appliqué all the designs with navy floss and the basic blanket stitch. This would be a quick project to machine blanket stitch because no thread color changes are required.

4 Quilt pillow: Layer the pillow top, batting, and backing; baste. Quilt by hand or machine around all the designs and echo quilt ¼" from the designs, Hawaiian-style.

5 Finish pillow: Construct lapped pillow back with 11" by 15" rectangles (page 25). Lap pillow backs to form 15" square with raw edges on the outside. Pin wrong sides together. Bind with stuffed binding following the directions on pages 23–24.

Posy pattern page 91.

Heart-Felt Wool Appliqué — *Lorinda Lie*

Let's Celebrate! Projects
Christmas Joy Pillow

by Sue Clemens

Materials

- Four 8" squares felted wool: two squares color A, one square color B
- 15" square of felted red and green wool plaid for pillow top
- Scraps of wool for appliqué and tongues
- ½ yd. cotton for lapped pillow back
- Embroidery floss
- Three red buttons for holly berries
- Freezer paper
- 14" pillow form

Patterns

Small Holly Leaf, page 75
Tongue, page 90
Alphabet, pages 101–107

Christmas Joy Pillow

Beginner level

14" pillow

Celebrate the Christmas season with a folk-art pillow. This quick and easy pillow would make a great gift. The pillow shown is appliquéd with the basic blanket stitch and is not quilted. The giant fringe is a typical finish used in old penny rugs. The fringe pieces are called "tongues," no doubt because of their size and shape.

Variations

- *Embroider letters with fancy stitches.*
- *Quilt the pillow, following the directions for the Quilted Pillow Top with Tongues on page 26–27.*
- *Make a wallhanging instead of a pillow. Put tongues on the bottom edge only.*
- *Make a pillow or wallhanging to celebrate occasions such as a birth, graduation, or wedding. Instead of holly leaves, use a baby rattle, mortar board, or wedding bells. Use either "JOY" or the initials of the person you are celebrating.*

Pillow Assembly

1 Prepare wool: If you are new to wool quilts, be sure to read Learning the Basics, pages 8–28, for directions on felting wool, and tips for how to work with it by hand or machine.

2 Appliqué top: Trace the letters "J," "O," and "Y" and the holly leaves on freezer paper. Cut out the pieces and press them on scraps of felted wool.

Arrange the letters and leaves on the pillow top and appliqué them in place by hand or machine with the basic blanket stitch. Add the "holly berry" buttons.

3 Prepare tongues: Cut out 36 tongues and blanket stitch around the edge of each one, leaving the straight ends unstitched (page 26). This step must be done by hand.

4 Finish pillow: Follow the directions on page 25 for a lapped pillow back and the directions on page 26 for finishing an unquilted pillow top with tongues.

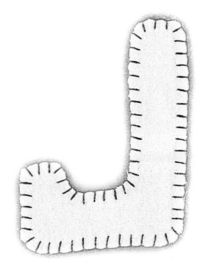

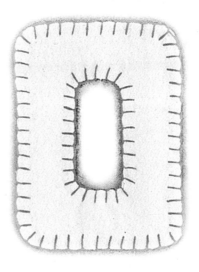

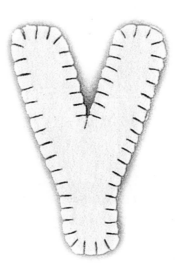

Patterns for letters on pages 101–107.

Let's Celebrate! Projects
Quilter's Crossword Quilt

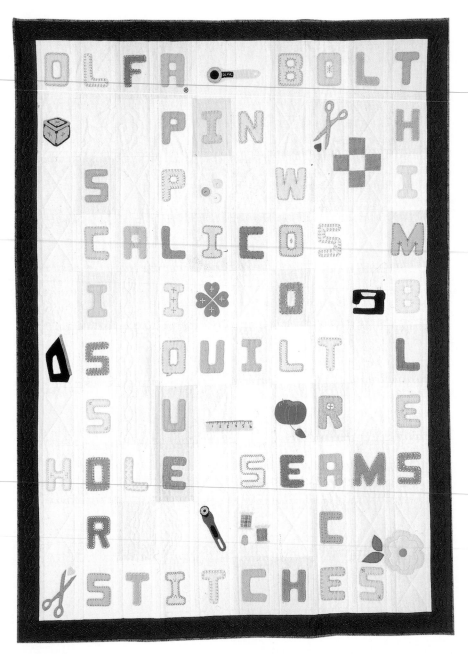

by Lorinda Lie

Quilter's Crossword Quilt

Intermediate/advanced level – The stitches are somewhat more challenging, particularly on the letter shapes.
55" x 75" topper or nap quilt
5" x 7" finished block

Quilters are such generous people. Isn't it time to celebrate and make a quilt just for you? Don't peek at the
photograph yet. Take a few minutes to work the puzzle
before beginning the quilt. QUILTER'S CROSSWORD is a real
crossword puzzle that includes your favorite quilting
terms and some tools, too.

When you have worked the puzzle, look at the picture.
All the wool is from recycled garments, including the
outer border. The fancy blanket stitch variations are fun to
do and make the quilt one you will never tire of seeing.

Variations

- *Appliqué the letters with the basic blanket stitch.*
- *Use navy or black wool for the background. Use
  bright colors, such as red, green, fuchsia, purple, and
  blue for letters.*
- *Make a crossword of your own in a different theme.
  Use family names or adapt a favorite crossword puz-
  zle. Try to cover the top fairly evenly and still inter-
  twine all the words crossword-style.*
- *Add a wider border to make a futon- or full-sized quilt.
  Remember, the larger your quilt, the heavier it will be.*

Crossword Puzzle

Across

1. Brand name of one rotary cutting tool.
2. Unit of fabric before it is cut and sold.
3. Used to fasten pieces of fabric together
   before sewing.
6. Cotton fabrics used in quilts are sometimes
   called _____.
9. A "fabric sandwich" that is stitched through
   all the layers.
11. What a moth makes in wool.
12. To unsew the wool garments, you must take
    out the _____.
13. Most of the time you want these to be nice
    and tiny.

Down

2. To stitch designs to the surface of a block.
4. These are used to protect your fingers
   when quilting.
6. Traditional tools for cutting fabric.
7. Fabric spun from sheep's hair.
10. To draw over a design using thin paper
    or plastic to see the shape underneath.

Materials

- Five to nine white and cream wool garments, equivalent to
  3½ yds. white wool. (Colors don't have to match.)
- Four or five pastel garments, equivalent to ⅝ yd. of pastel wool
- Felted wool scraps in colors to match specific tools
  (black, yellow, dark green, light gray, tan or camel, and purple)
- One pleated skirt or several of the same dark color, or ⅞ yd.
  new wool in a darker color for a narrow border
- 3½ yds. cotton for backing
- 1 yd. cotton for 3" double-fold, straight-grain binding
- Embroidery floss in assorted contrasting colors for letters,
  and matching colors for tools
- Batting. (80%/20% cotton/polyester in quilt pictured.)
- Freezer paper   • Masking tape
- Three large buttons in pastel colors for embellishment

Patterns

Hearts, page 78
Tools and Large Posy,
pages 85–88
Alphabet and Numbers,
pages 101–110

Quilt Assembly

1 Prepare wool: If you are new to wool quilts, be sure to read Learning the Basics, pages 8–28, for directions on felting wool, and tips for how to work with it by hand or machine.

2 Cut rectangles: Cut 100 rectangles, 6" x 8", from white wool.

3 Cut appliqué: Trace the letters needed on freezer paper, cut the shapes, and iron them on wool scraps. Letters do not need to be reversed when using freezer paper. To make the quilt pictured, you will need the following letters: 3 A, 2 B, 4 C, 4 E, 1 F, 3 H, 7 I, 6 L, 2 M, 1 N, 5 O, 2 P, 1 Q, 2 R, 8 S, 4 T, 2 U, 1 W.

Cut all 58 letters from assorted pastels. Cut approximately the same number of letters from each color, randomly scattering the colors across the quilt.

Cut tools from appropriate colors of wool, following the quilt picture. Also cut four hearts for heart block, four squares for nine patch, two mini hearts for scissors blocks, one large posy from three colors of pink, and posy leaves.

4 Appliqué blocks: Remove the freezer paper from the letters and center them, one to a block. They will be 2" from the top and bottom of each block. The distance from the sides will vary with each letter. Staple the letters in place on the background blocks with standard staples. Stapling makes it easier to embroider the letters without snagging your thread or having pins poke your fingers. Staple inside the stitching line in the center of each letter so the staples will not be in the way of the stitches.

Appliqué the blocks with fancy stitches in contrasting embroidery floss. See fancy stitch directions for how-tos and ideas, on page 19. Use two colors of floss when sewing combination stitches.

The fancy stitches are slightly bigger than the normal blanket stitch. An average bite and distance may be as much as ¼", but this will vary with the stitch used. The corners on all the letters are rounded rather than sharp.

However, they will require some special treatment if you are using the fancy stitches. Start stitching in the middle of the longest side of each letter to give you a chance to get a feel for the rhythm of the stitch before dealing with corners. You may have to alter the stitch slightly to accommodate the corners.

Picture an imaginary center line running through the corner. The stitches made on one side of the center line need to be mirrored on the other side. Depending on the stitch and how you handle the corner, you may have room for a complete fancy stitch, or you may need to

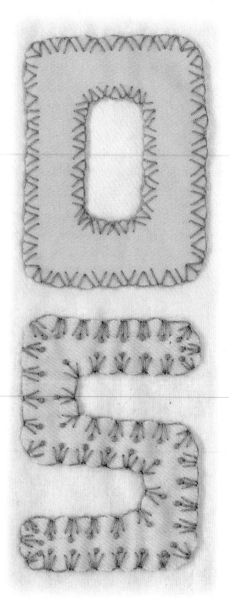

Use fancy stitches and contrasting floss to appliqué letters.

Heart-Felt Wool Appliqué — Lorinda Lie

abbreviate the stitch. Be creative. If symmetry is not your thing, don't worry about the corners. Keep stitching and let them happen as they will, folk-art style.

Follow the photograph and crossword grid for tool placement. Appliqué the tools with the basic blanket stitch and matching floss. You may have to wait to appliqué some tools until you have sewn several of the blocks together because the tools may span several blocks.

When all the appliqué is complete, remove the staples and arrange the blocks. Join the blocks in units of two, then units of four. Sew the units into sections, then sew the sections together to complete the quilt top. Pin blocks together carefully, then sew. Press seam allowances open. When joining four-block units and larger sections, pin on each side of the intersection to keep seams aligned. Stitch carefully, using a walking foot and reduced pressure on the presser foot. Support the weight of the quilt as you sew.

5 Add border: Cut strips 3½" wide along the grain of the garment or fabric. Piece the strips together with diagonal seams as necessary to make two 71" strips and two 56" strips. Mark ½" at the beginning and end of the two longest strips, for the seam allowances, and 7" intervals in between. Match the marks to the seam intersections and pin. This method will ensure correct length and fit. Support the weight of the quilt as you sew the long seams. Press seam allowances open.

Mark the top and bottom borders 3" from both ends of the shorter strips and at 5" intervals in between. Match the marks to the seam intersections and pin. Sew the top and bottom borders in place. Press seam allowances open.

6 Mark quilt: Choose a variety of quilting motifs from commercial templates or design your own for some of the blank squares. Four-inch designs will fit in a single block. Larger ones may fit across several blocks. Appliqué shapes, such as the large posy, can also be used as quilting designs.

The white wool can be easily marked with a turquoise water-soluble pen. Test all markers on your fabrics before using them. Wait until you are ready to quilt the outer border before marking it because this will have to be marked with soapstone or chalk.

If you would prefer not to mark directly on the wool, use another method for marking quilts, such as tape or an adhesive paper. Wait to mark the border until you are ready to quilt it.

7 Layer quilt: To prepare the backing fabric, trim the selvages. Cut the piece in half lengthwise and piece the two lengths together (see Figure 28 page 28). Layer the backing, batting, and top, and baste the layers together and baste layers together.

8 Quilt: Quilt with natural-colored quilting thread ¾" from all seams using ¾" masking tape as a guide. Quilt around each letter and tool. Quilt a variety of designs in some of the empty spaces, quilt the remaining empty spaces with an "X." Use a cable design (page 86) on the border. Make a plastic template from cable design and mark the border with soapstone, chalk or a pouncing tool as you work. Hairspray will help preserve the marks, or use adhesive paper.

9 Finish edges: Cut 3"-wide, straight-grain binding strips from cotton fabric. Piece strips together diagonally, as necessary. Press the pieced strip in half, wrong sides together. Sew the binding on the front of the quilt, mitering the corners. Hand stitch in place on the back. Label your quilt and enjoy.

Collecting Wool

To find wool for this quilt, look at ladies pants, suits, and skirts. Pants are a good source of white wool and can be cut economically for the rectangular shape. It takes some hunting, but wool garments in pastel colors are out there. They are the January colors for ladies suits. Don't worry if all the whites aren't the same weave or color. They will blend together and lend subtle interest to the quilt.

Part Three: **Patterns**

Detail from FRED'S QUILT

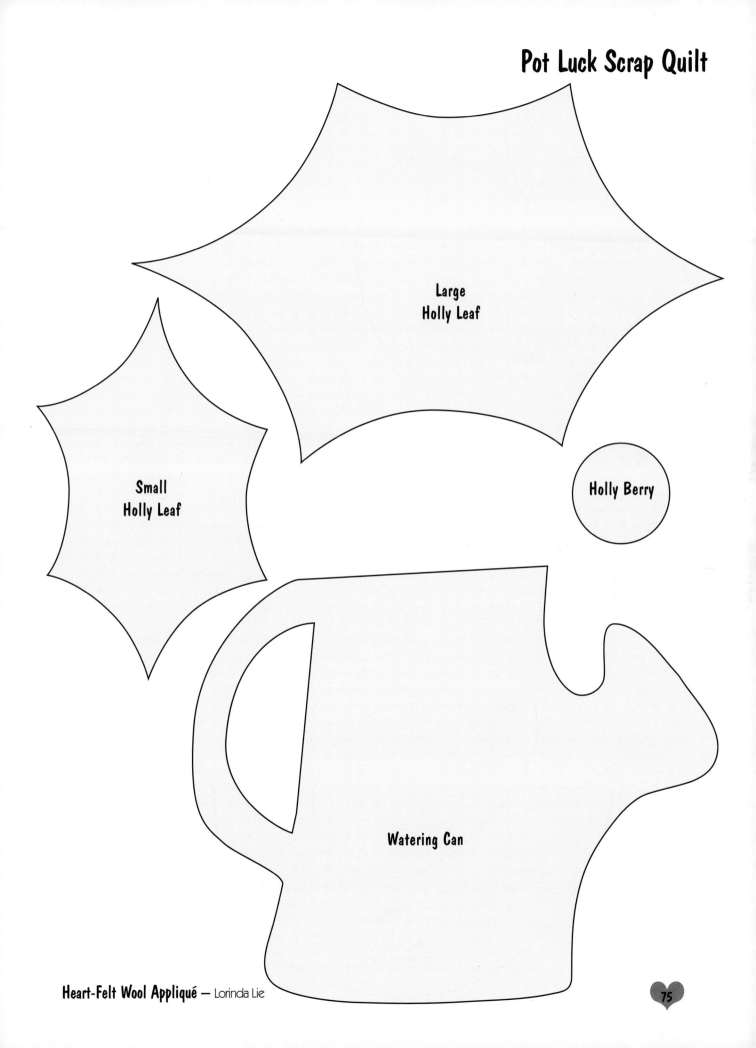

Large
Holly Leaf

Small
Holly Leaf

Holly Berry

Watering Can

Pot Luck Scrap Quilt

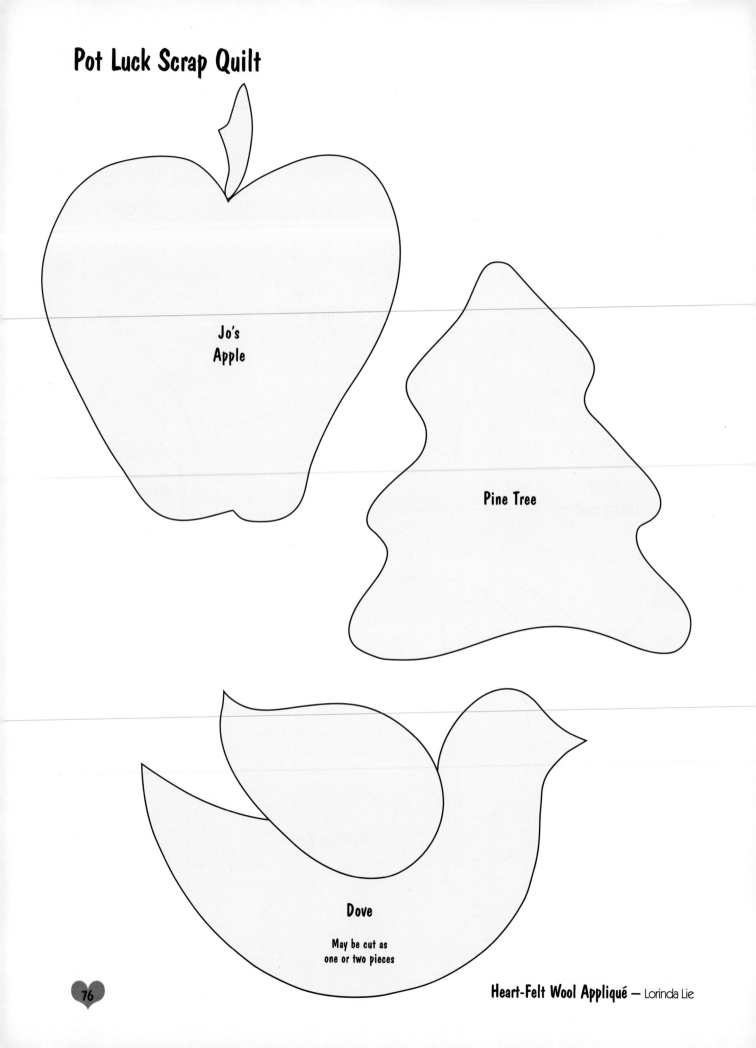

Jo's
Apple

Pine Tree

Dove

May be cut as
one or two pieces

Heart-Felt Wool Appliqué — Lorinda Lie

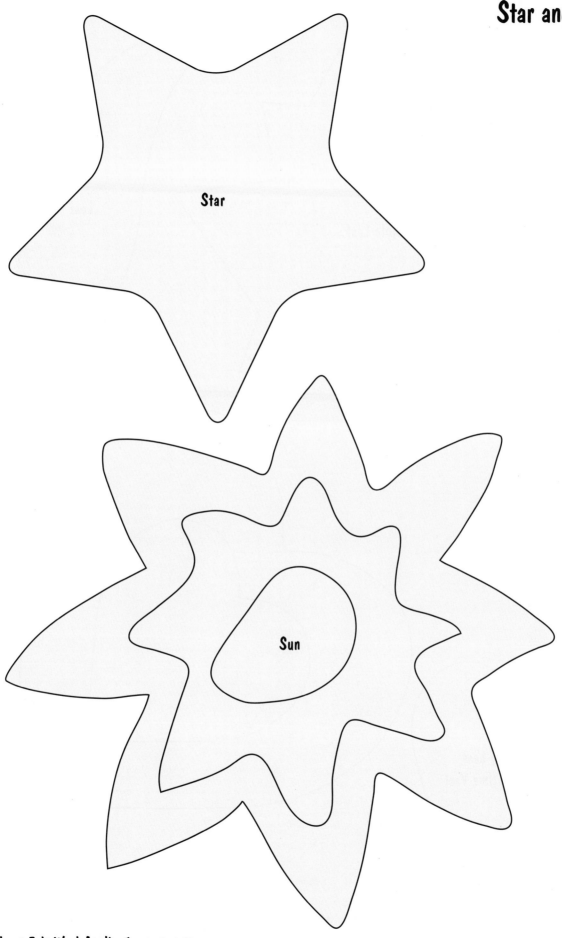

Star

Sun

Heart-Felt Wool Appliqué — *Lorinda Lie*

Leaves and Hearts

Leaf

Maple Leaf

Posy Leaf
Springtime Vest

Heart and Hand

© Cookie Cutter Collectibles

Heart-Felt Wool Appliqué — *Lorinda Lie*

Heart Patterns

Primary Bulbs Quilting

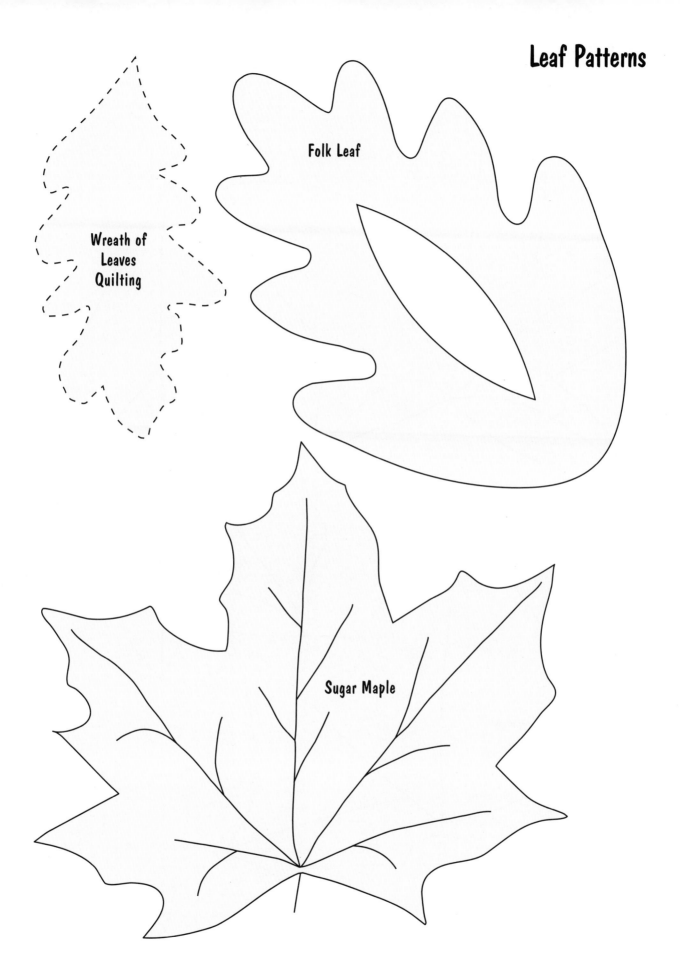

Wreath of
Leaves
Quilting

Folk Leaf

Sugar Maple

Leaf Patterns

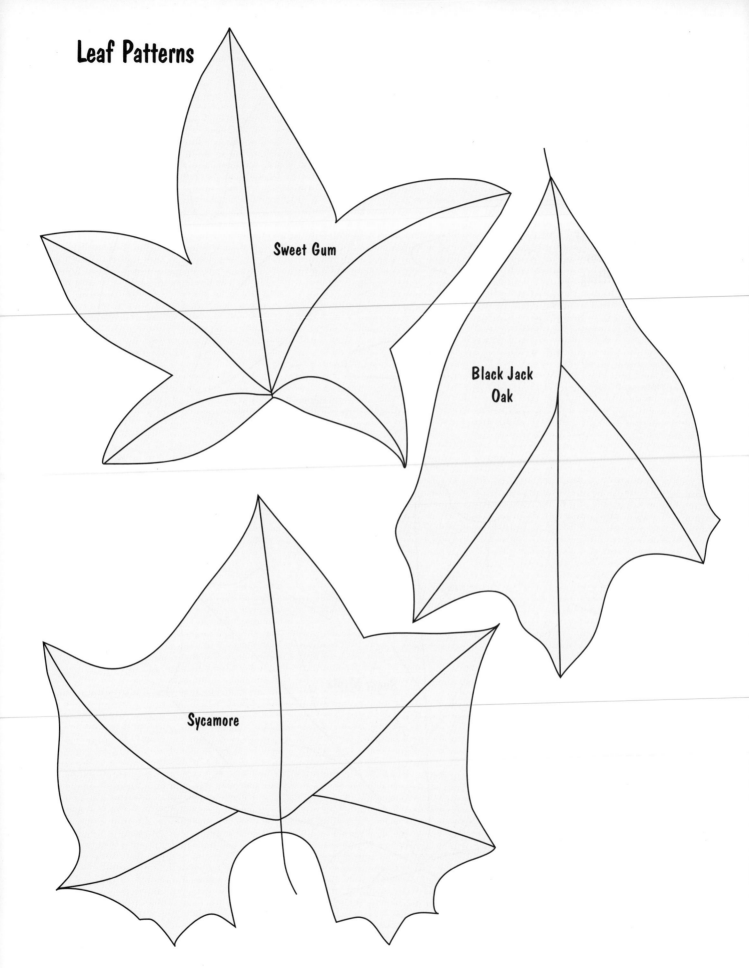

Sweet Gum

Black Jack Oak

Sycamore

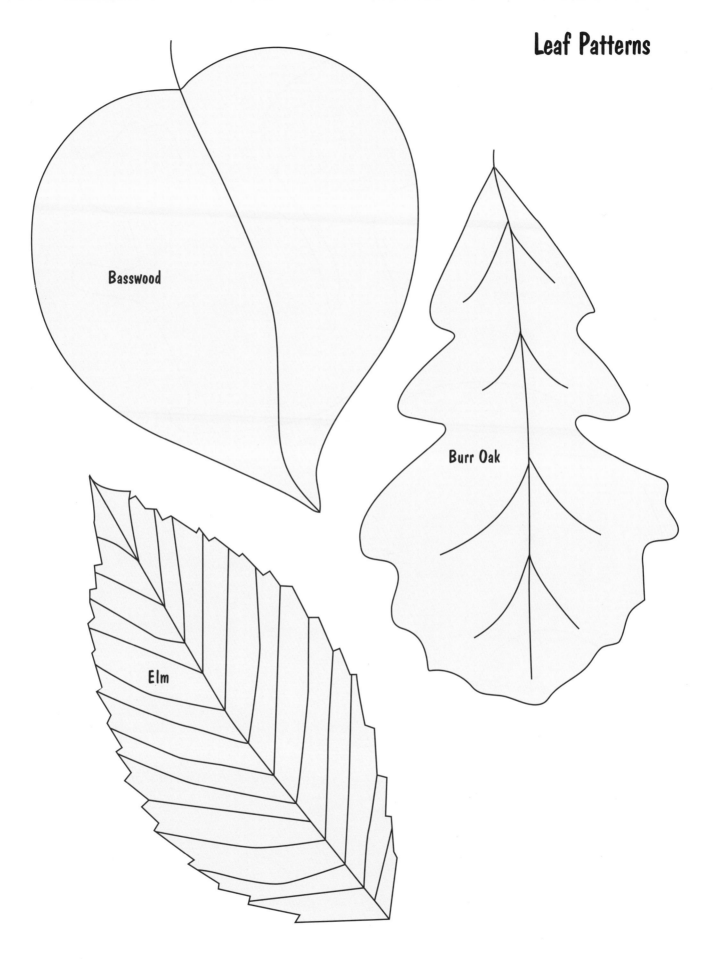

Basswood

Burr Oak

Elm

Squirrel Patterns

Any pattern can be
reduced or reversed.

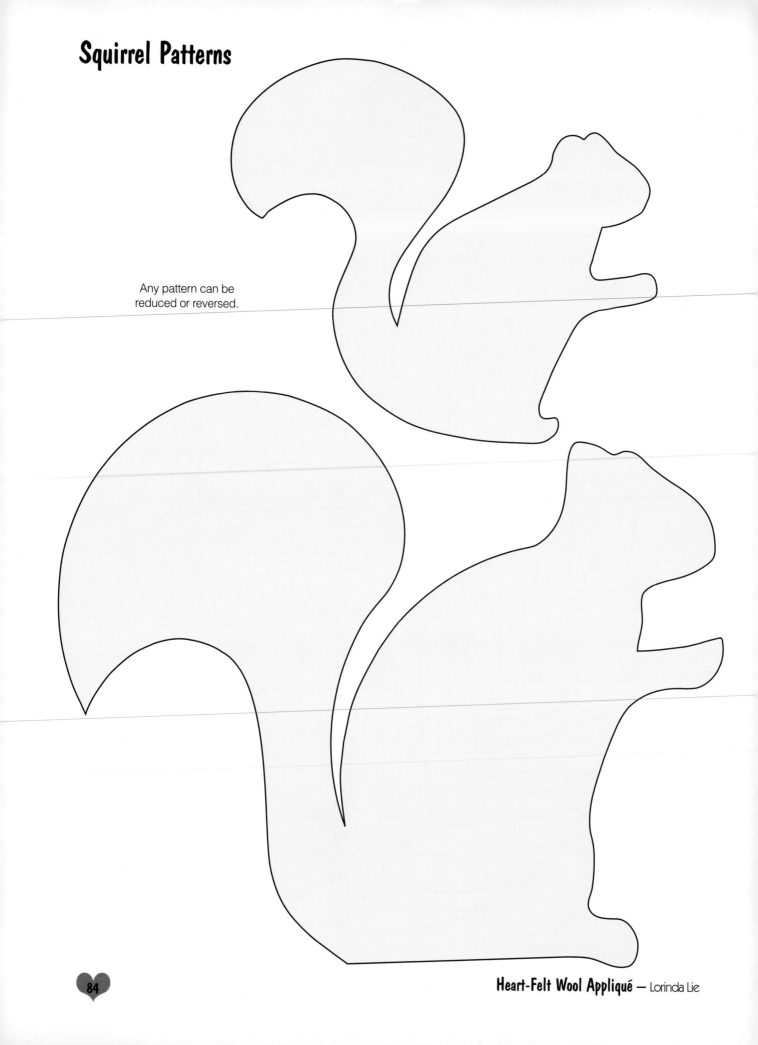

Heart-Felt Wool Appliqué — Lorinda Lie

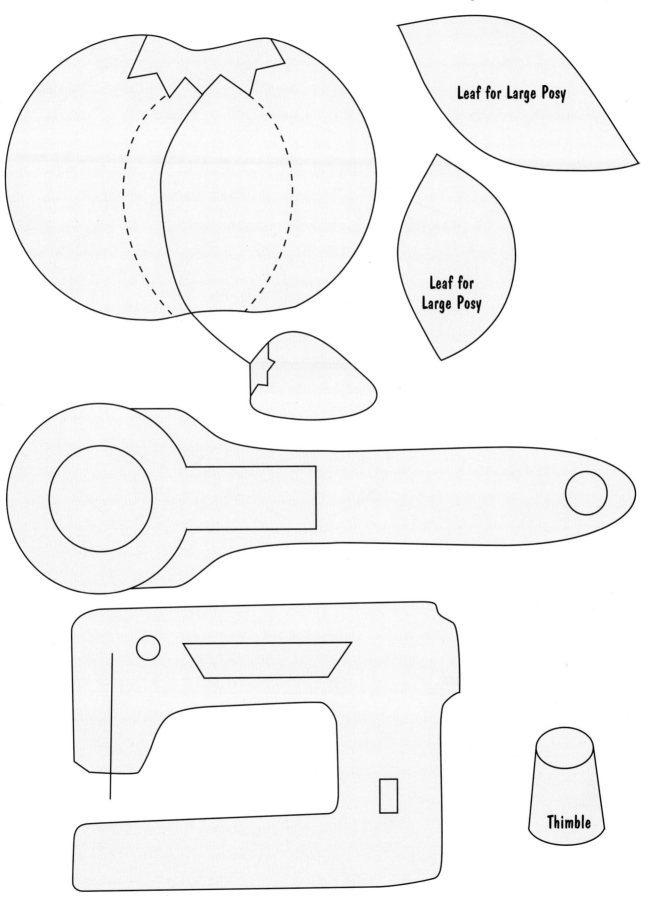

Leaf for Large Posy

Leaf for
Large Posy

Thimble

Heart-Felt Wool Appliqué — Lorinda Lie

Quilter's Crossword

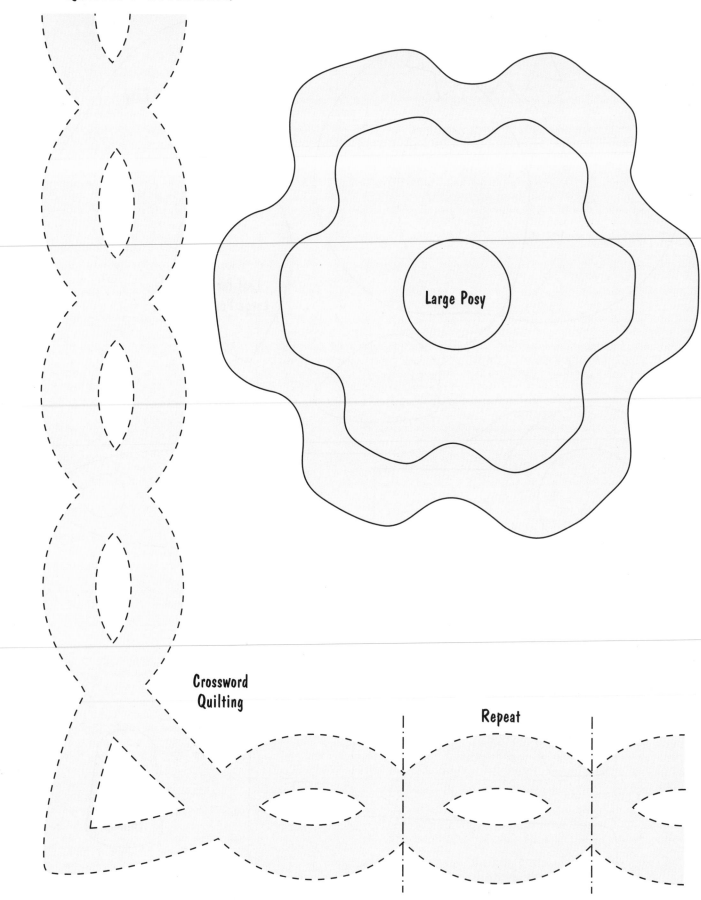

Large Posy

Crossword
Quilting

Repeat

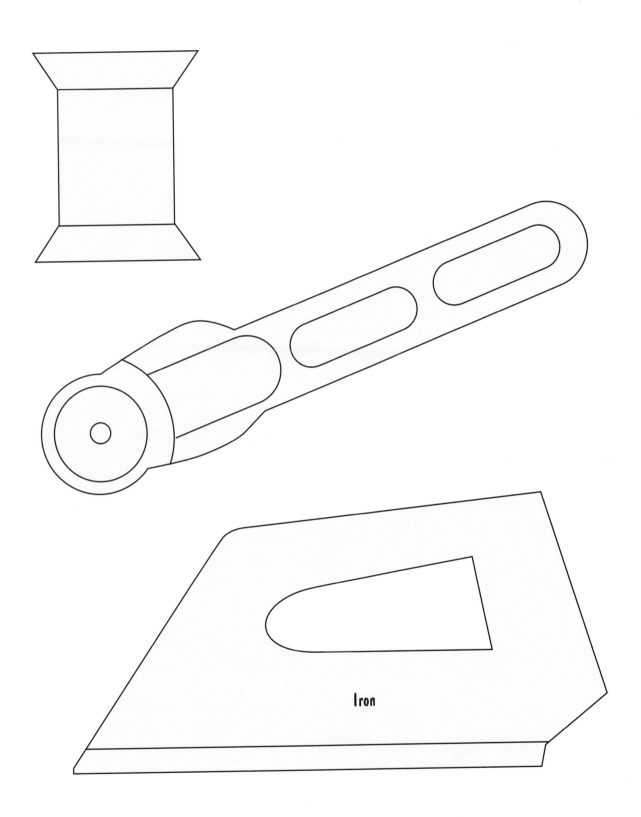

Iron

Quilter's Crossword

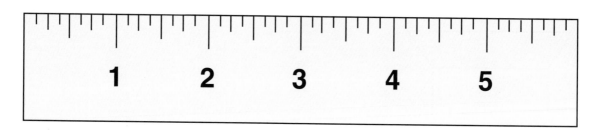

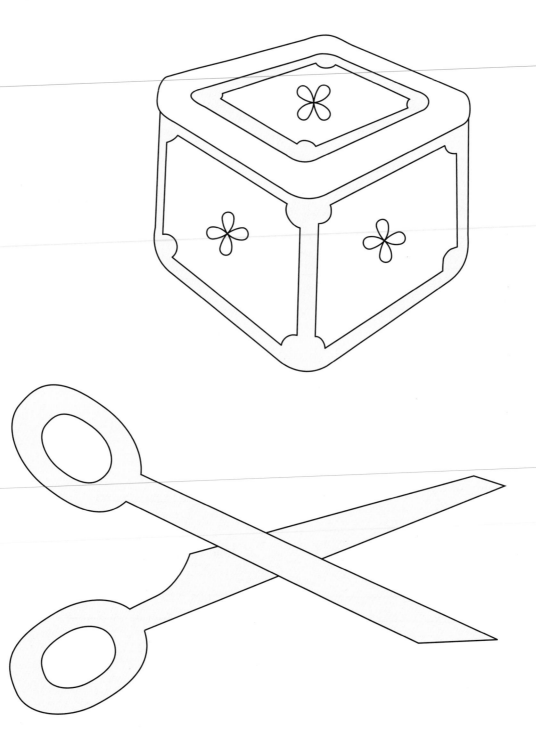

Tulip Garden

E

D
Tulip Garden

Dr

I
Tulip Garden

H
Tulip Garden

Heart-Felt Wool Appliqué — Lorinda Lie

Tulip Garden and Cat

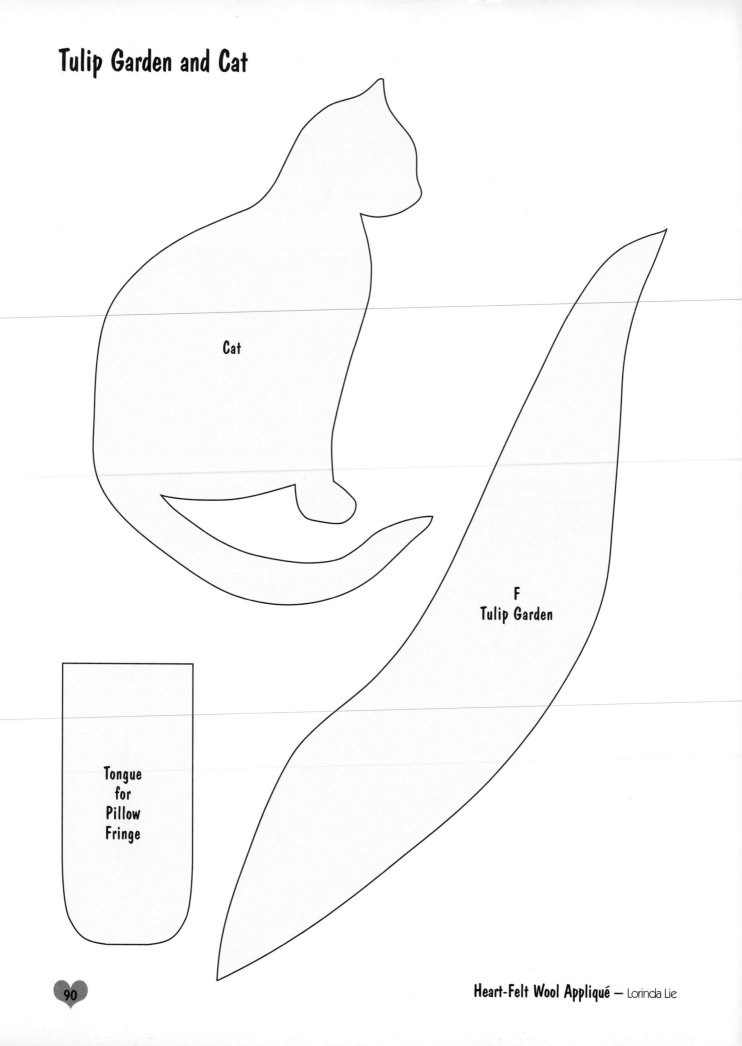

Cat

F
Tulip Garden

Tongue
for
Pillow
Fringe

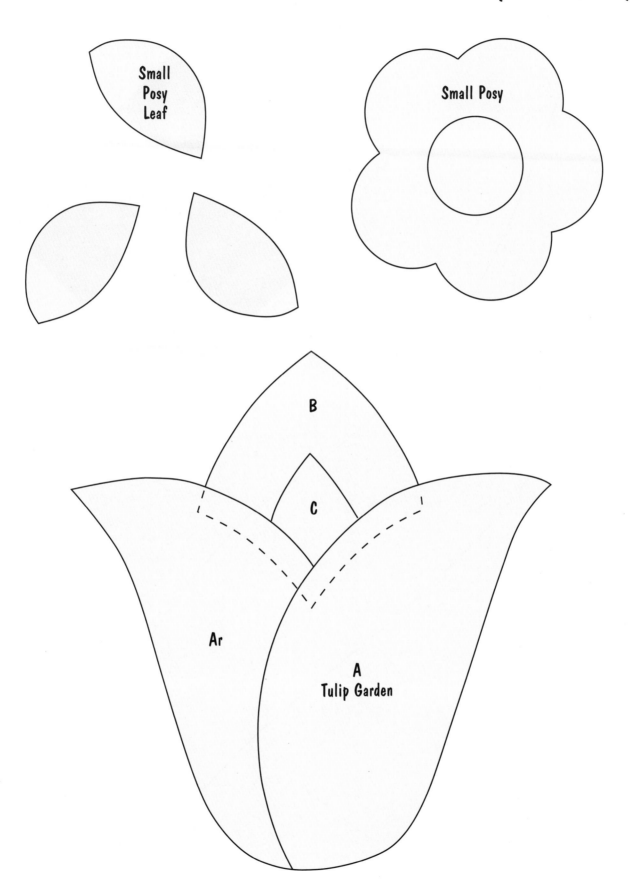

Small
Posy
Leaf

Small Posy

B

C

Ar

A
Tulip Garden

Tulip Garden

G
Tulip Garden

Fan Dance Quilting Pattern

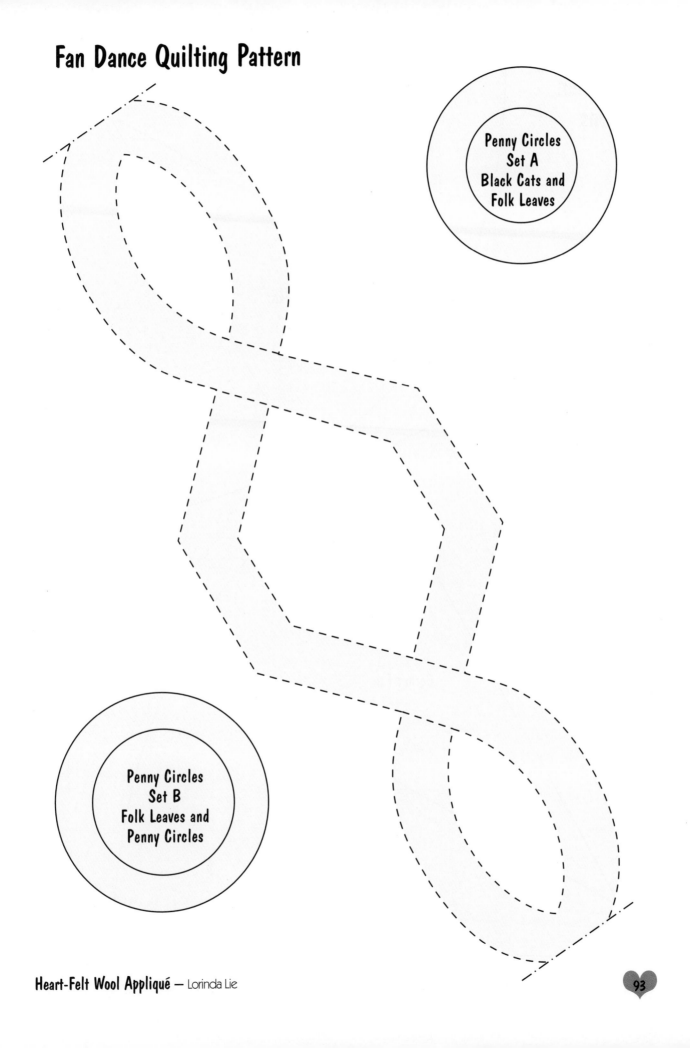

Penny Circles
Set A
Black Cats and
Folk Leaves

Penny Circles
Set B
Folk Leaves and
Penny Circles

Heart-Felt Wool Appliqué — *Lorinda Lie*

Fan Dance Foundation Patterns

Paper foundations include ½" seam allowance on straight sides

C

Center Fan

B

A

A

B

Corner Fan

C

Heart-Felt Wool Appliqué — Lorinda Lie

Fan Dance Quilting Patterns

Fold and Cut Patterns

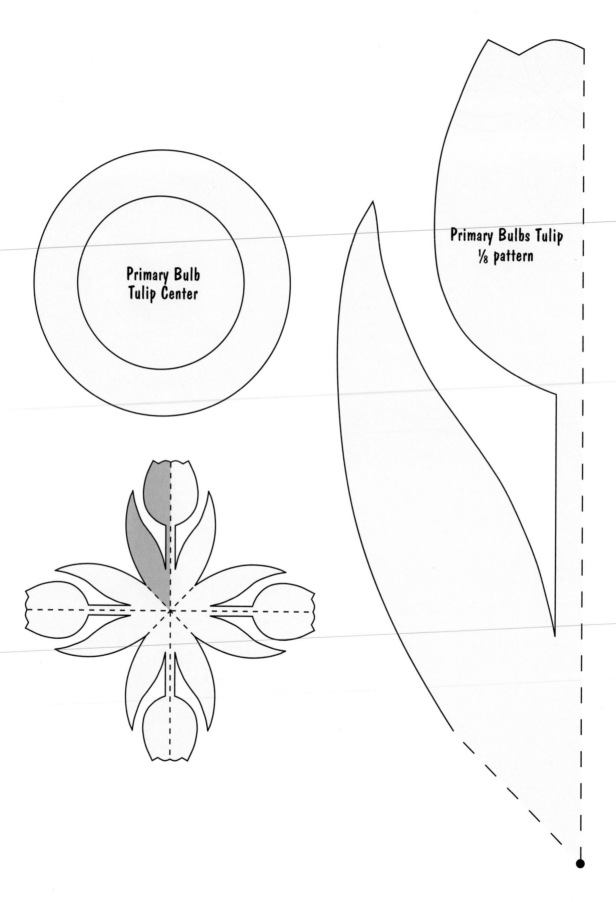

Primary Bulb
Tulip Center

Primary Bulbs Tulip
⅛ pattern

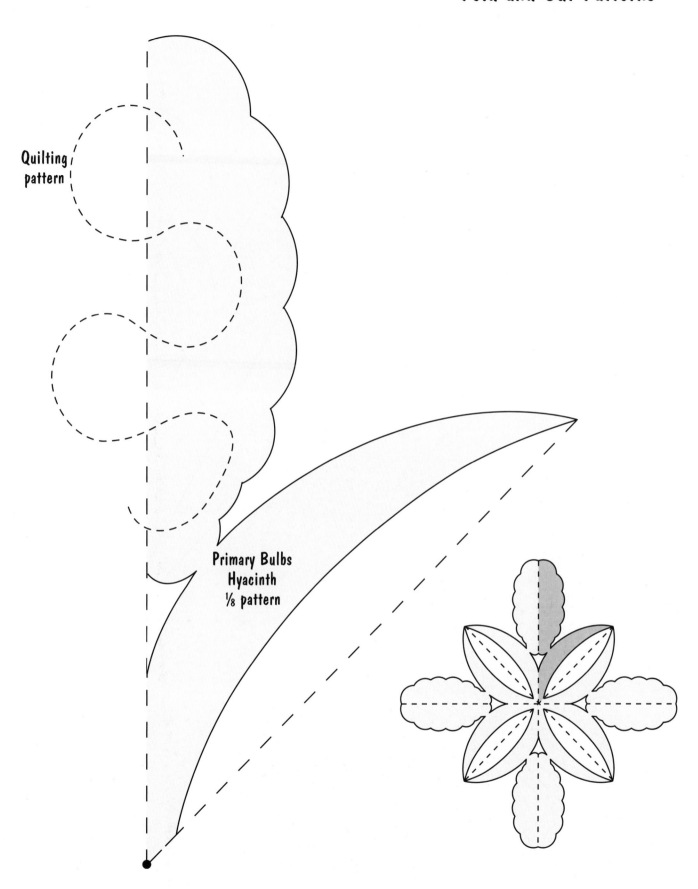

Quilting
pattern

Primary Bulbs
Hyacinth
⅛ pattern

Heart-Felt Wool Appliqué — *Lorinda Lie*

Fold and Cut Patterns

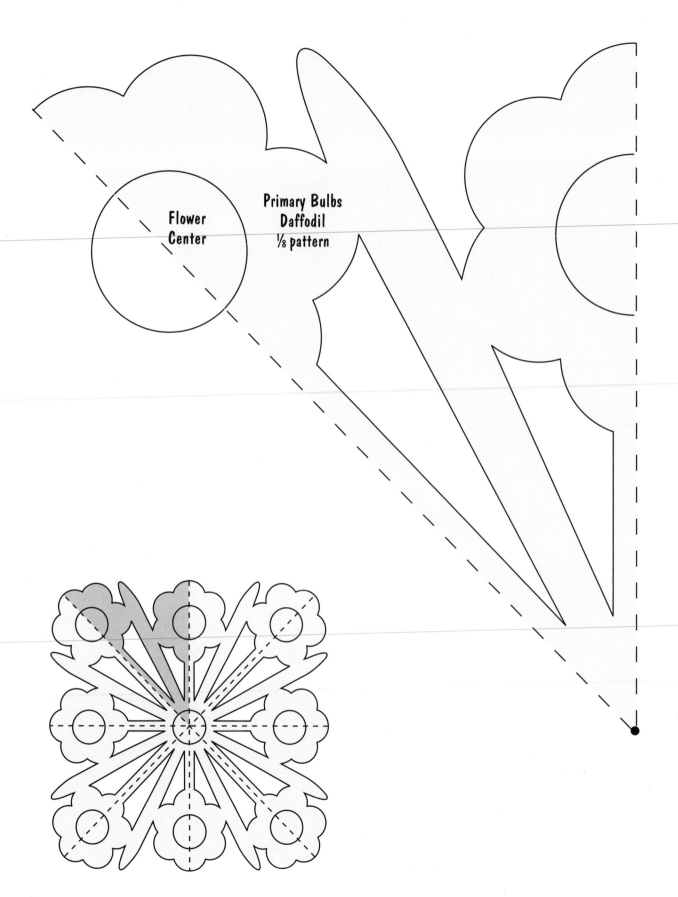

Flower
Center

Primary Bulbs
Daffodil
⅛ pattern

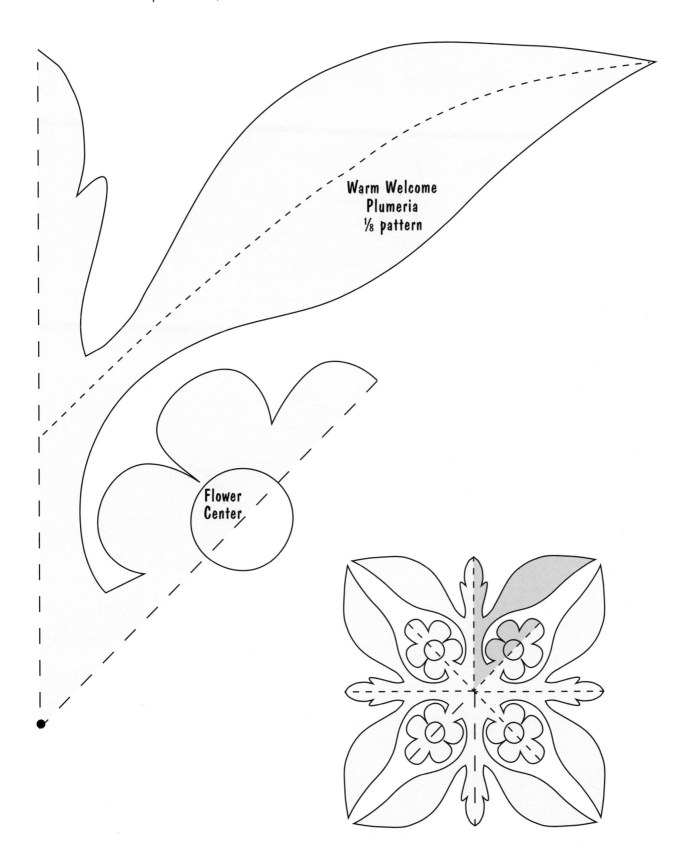

The Plumeria and Pineapple patterns
are used with permission from
HAWAIIAN QUILTING
by Elizabeth Root, Dover Publications.

Fold and Cut Patterns

Warm Welcome
Plumeria
⅛ pattern

Flower
Center

Heart-Felt Wool Appliqué — Lorinda Lie

Fold and Cut Patterns

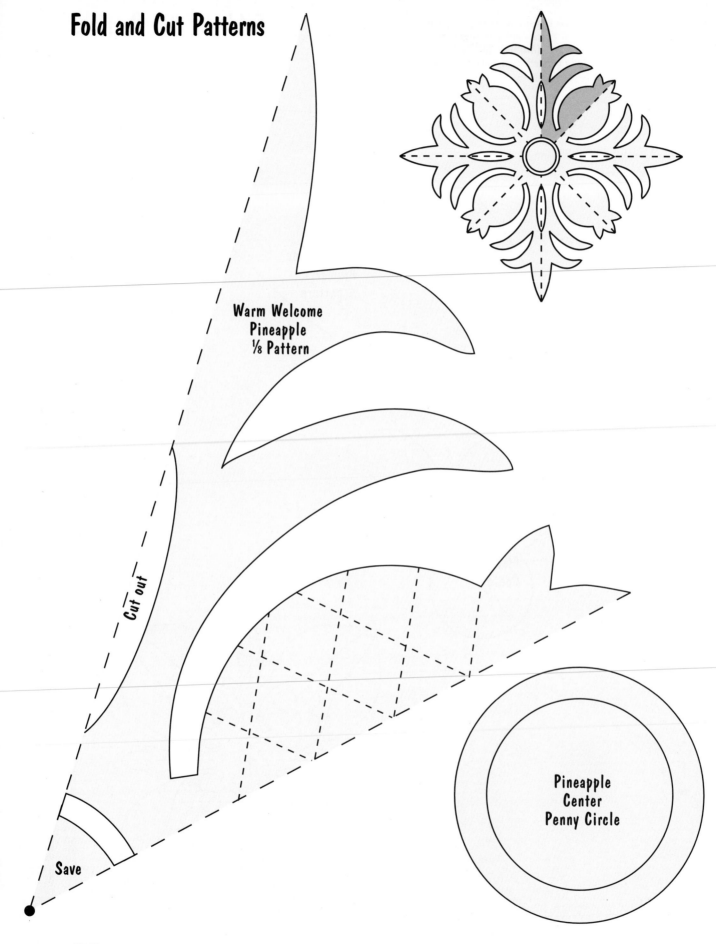

Warm Welcome
Pineapple
⅛ Pattern

Cut out

Save

Pineapple
Center
Penny Circle

Letters and Numbers

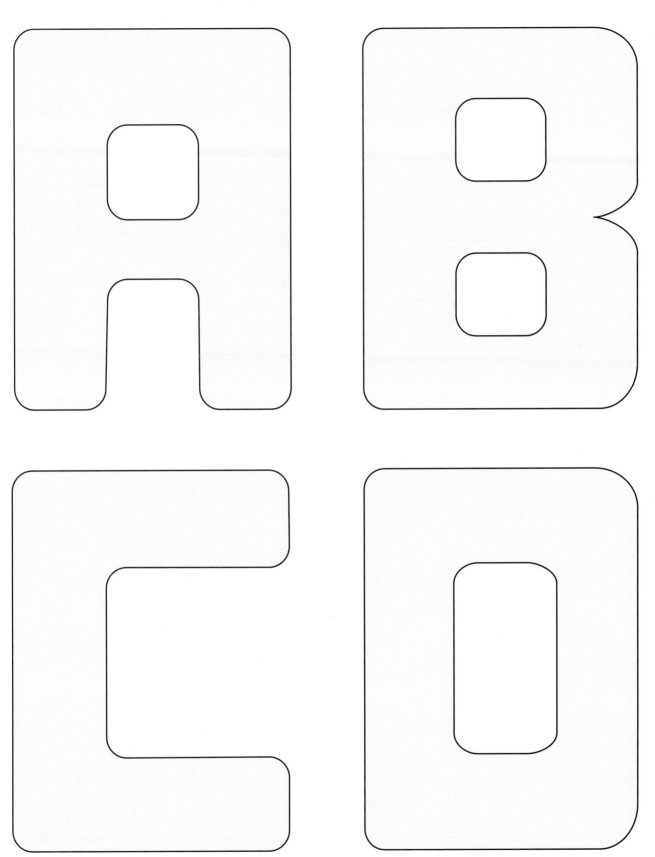

Jo's Alphabet © 1996 Shared Ideas

Heart-Felt Wool Appliqué — Lorinda Lie

Letters and Numbers

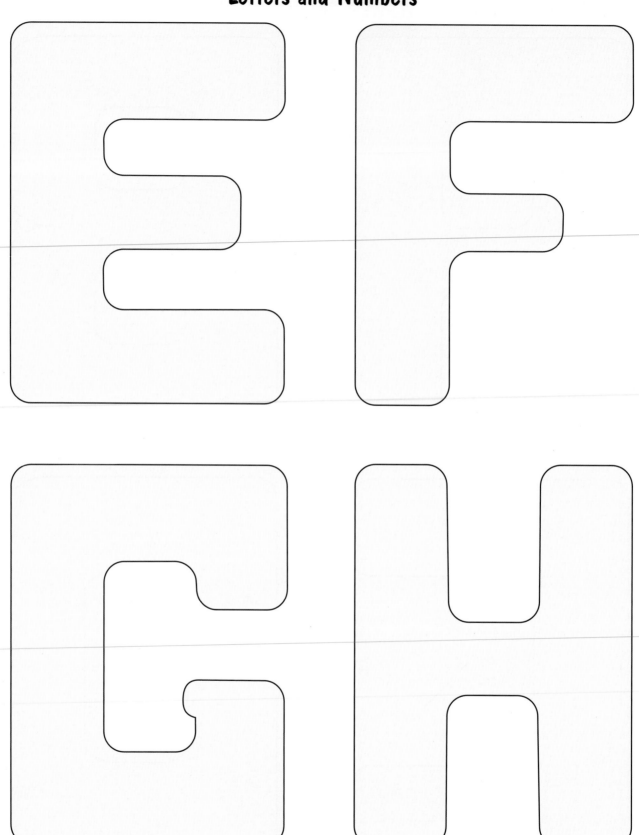

Heart-Felt Wool Appliqué — Lorinda Lie

Letters and Numbers

Jo's Alphabet © 1996 Shared Ideas

Heart-Felt Wool Appliqué — Lorinda Lie

Letters and Numbers

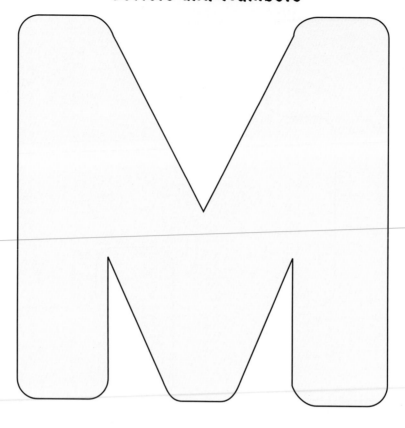

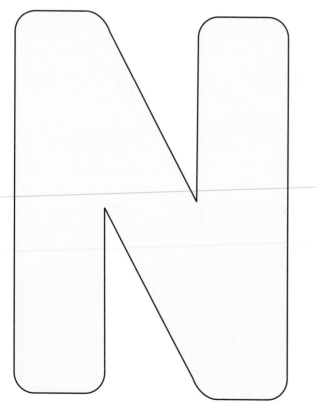

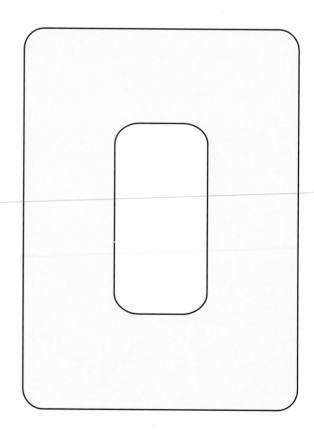

Jo's Alphabet © 1996 Shared Ideas

Heart-Felt Wool Appliqué — Lorinda Lie

Letters and Numbers

Jo's Alphabet © 1996 Shared Ideas

Heart-Felt Wool Appliqué — *Lorinda Lie*

ABCDEFGHIJKLMNOPQRSTUVWXYZ1234567890

105

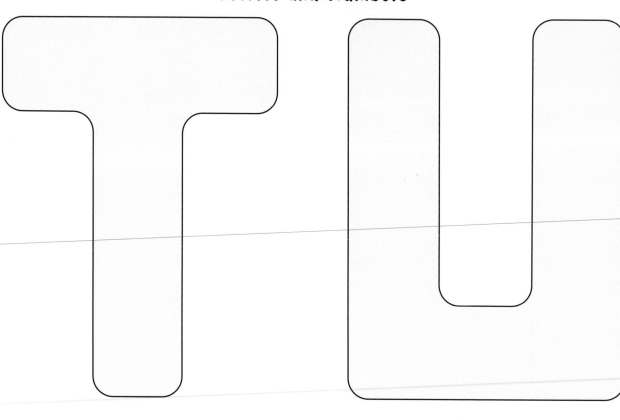

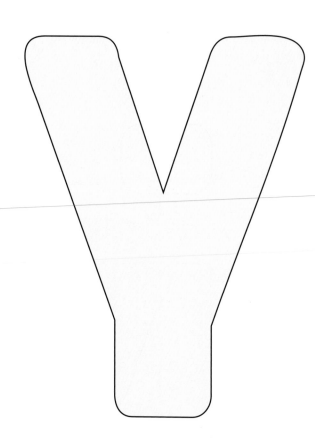

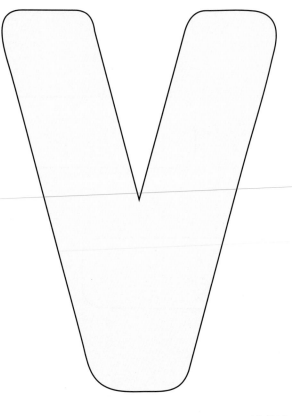

Jo's Alphabet © 1996 Shared Ideas

Heart-Felt Wool Appliqué — Lorinda Lie

Letters and Numbers

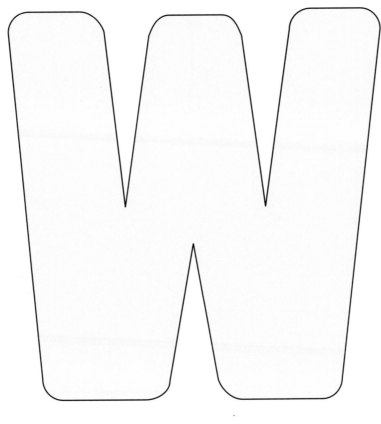

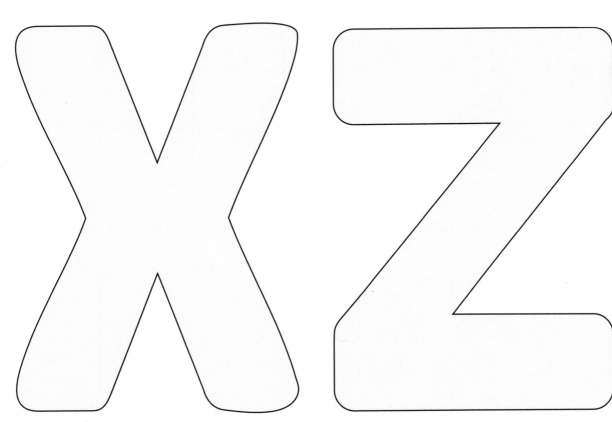

Jo's Alphabet © 1996 Shared Ideas

Heart-Felt Wool Appliqué — *Lorinda Lie*

Letters and Numbers

Jo's Alphabet © 1996 Shared Ideas

Heart-Felt Wool Appliqué — Lorinda Lie

Letters and Numbers

5 b

7 8

Heart-Felt Wool Appliqué — Lorinda Lie

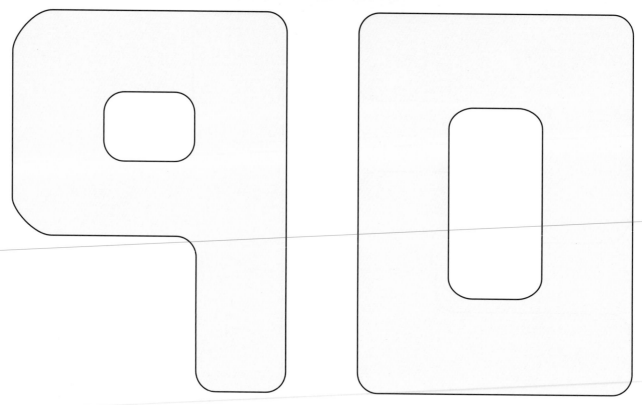

Jo's Alphabet © 1996 Shared Ideas

Bibliography

Brandt, Janet Carija. *Wool-on-Wool Folk Art Quilts*, That Patchwork Place, Bothwell, WA, 1995.

Doak, Carol. *Easy Reversible Vests*, That Patchwork Place, Bothwell, WA, 1995.

Enthoven, Jacquelyne. *The Stitches of Creative Embroidery*, Van Nostrand Reinhold Company, New York, NY, 1964.

Parker, Julie. *All about Wool, a Fabric Dictionary and Swatchbook Vol. IV*, Rain City Publishing, Seattle, WA, 1996.

Root, Elizabeth. *Hawaiian Quilting*, Dover Publications, New York, NY, 1989.

Shackelford, Anita. *Appliqué with Folded Cutwork*, American Quilter's Society, Paducah, KY, 1999.

Thomas, Mary. *Dictionary of Embroidery Stitches*, Gramercy Publishing Co., New York, NY, 1935.

Wagner, Debra. *Traditional Quilts, Today's Techniques*, Krause Publications, Lola, WI, 1997.

Resources

Cookie Cutter Collectibles, 120 Linker Rd., Dover, AR 72837; 800-711-8544

Hobbs Bonded Fibers, PO Box 2521, Waco, TX 76702-2521; 254-741-0040; Thermore™ Batting

Heart-Felt Wool Appliqué — Lorinda Lie

About the Author

Her grandmother's quilts were brought out for special occasions. Her dad could fix anything and in fact made all their kitchen cupboards. Her mom was always making something, from candles to cookies to clothes. So it seemed natural for Lorinda to grow up valuing creativity and making things with her hands. She sewed, knitted, and embroidered before discovering quilting in the late '70s. While it was an art she knew she would take up one day, it took a push from a friend who wanted to exchange quilt blocks by mail to finally get her started. The quilt she made from those blocks is still in the frame! It is the process she enjoys more than the finished product.

After teaching in a variety of elementary-school settings and teaching substance-abuse prevention to people of all ages, Lorinda turned her teaching skills to quilting. She joined a guild 1982 and was soon presenting programs and teaching workshops for the members. She has been teaching outside her guild since the late '80s with her partner, Jo Fifield, including a wool workshop at the American Quilter's Society Quilt Show in 1998. Having moved twice in the last two years, she now teaches solo, as well as writing, designing, and working part time in a bookstore.

Lorinda enjoys original design, bright colors, and the folk-art look. She often combines appliqué with pieced work. Having begun sewing by making her own clothes, she frequently applies her quilting skills to clothing design and decoration. Her clothing and quilts have won many awards at local shows.

AQS books are known worldwide for timely topics, clear writing, beautiful color photos, and accurate illustrations and patterns. This is only a small selection of the books available from your local bookseller, quilt shop or public library.

#5336 $22.95

#55916 $18.95

#5106 $16.95

#3929 $16.95

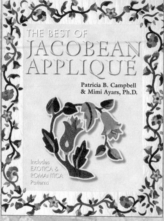

#5588 $24.95

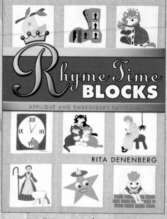

#5711 $19.95

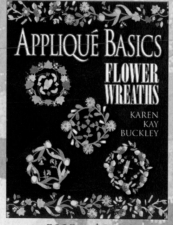

#5335 $21.95

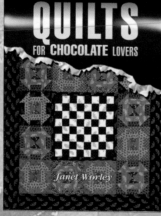

#5758 $19.95

#5705 $22.95